MW00929846

Survivors of the Coronavirus

Survivors of the Coronavirus
How We Escaped This Deadly Virus

SARA J. PRICE

XULON PRESS

Xulon Press
2301 Lucien Way #415
Maitland, FL 32751
407.339.4217
www.xulonpress.com

© 2020 by Sara J. Price

All rights reserved solely by the author. The author guarantees all
contents are original and do not infringe upon the legal rights of any
other person or work. No part of this book may be reproduced in any
form without the permission of the author. The views expressed in
this book are not necessarily those of the publisher.

Unless otherwise indicated, Scripture quotations taken from the King
James Version (KJV) – *public domain*.

Printed in the United States of America.

Paperback ISBN-13: 978-1-6322-1752-3
Hard Cover ISBN-13: 978-1-6322-1753-0
Ebook ISBN-13: 978-1-6322-1754-7

Dedication

I want to dedicate my book to the one who formed me in my mother's womb and who gave me life upon this Earth and life eternally. And He knew me by my name before I knew myself. And He gave me to my precious parents, Reverend Billy and Margaret Watson. Then He saved me and redeemed Me by His precious blood 2,000 years ago and called me His own. He filled me with a sweet spirit, and He loves me.

He gave me my sweet husband, Donnie Price, with whom I have shared forty-eight years in the union of marriage, and God did not stop there. He went on and bless us with three children and seven grandchildren.

God let every one of us live in this horrible sickness that has come up on the land, my God has been faithful. We owe Him our eternal life forever and ever and ever. We love You, Lord Jesus Christ, and we praise You. I dedicate my book to You. Thank You for your faithfulness and thank you for your sweet love and thank you for saving my sweet Donnie's life. I, Sara J. Price, give You honor, reverence, love, and praise for eternity.

I dedicate this book to You, my sweet Lord Jesus Christ.

Acknowledgments

I want to acknowledge my sweet family that stood by us through this crisis and loved us so much with many tears and prayers, fasting, and seeking God and belief that we were coming out this crisis. I need to say to every one of you I've never been so proud in my life how you strengthened your courage and your prayers. We love you forever, you who are my family that God has given me, and I am so proud calling you my family. You stood together as a family, and you stood strong, believing that God was going to bring us out of this, and He did. Thank you. I want the also to acknowledge the power in prayer that came from the Christian Church in Massachusetts.

Our church family stood with us and fasted and prayed and cried before God. Your prayers were answered. God brought your pastors out of this storm called coronavirus. I love every single one of you. God is faithful.

Contents

INTRODUCTION:

The Scriptures Confirming God's DNA in You

How did we survive? How did it happen? We survived the worst pandemic that our generation or world has ever seen. This disease is called the coronavirus (COVID-19). All the world was in a panic at the same time; the world was in lockdown at the same time, and then there was an awakening by many Christians all over the world, calling out to God, repenting, and singing "God help us." The world is still waiting to know what happened in China.

This disease would make a person experience what it is like to come close to death. This sickness feels like more than we can ever bear, above anything in our life we've ever experienced before. To conquer it, your faith must be very strong, never wavering in fear. Thousands were and still are dying, which is why the world was wrapped up in fear and in such a panic. Everyone was saying, "What in the world is going on? Lord, help us." The only hope you ever will have is to be wrapped up in *faith* in God.

While fighting COVID-19, we were wrapped up in faith knowing that God is faithful.

The DNA of God is inside of you when you know the scriptures from the Word of God, the Bible. The Word of God is real. You must only believe because "All things are possible to them that believe" Mark 9:23 That verse will help you believe in the spoken Word of God. Thank God, He sent His Word, and His Word will never fail.

I'm giving you some scriptures to help you be strong. If you're ever exposed to any type of sickness or even a pandemic, you will be strong enough to believe His Word and act on it by faith quickly, without fear! Then you will see results in your life and in your family's life. You will see God move powerfully in your own blood, called the DNA of God inside of you. The spoken word will heal your sickness, your diseases, and the devil will flee suddenly.

Fear is not of God, it is from the pit of hell. You have to make that spirit go back to hell and send that spirit to death through the name of the Lord Jesus Christ.

APRIL 12, 2020

April 12, 2020, is the day I started writing this book with the experiences we've had. I had just been released from the hospital, and I felt I had to write this book. Before I begin our testimonies, I want to give you the scriptures that helped me so you can be strengthened. And we give Him all the glory.

I have used a special saying for years in my ministry: I cannot do anything, but I pitch out the barrels of the anointing, and Jesus Christ does all the work, and he gets all the glory! Amen.

I want your family to be healed and set free and give God the glory too, as you are healed.

SCRIPTURES TO LIVE BY

I always have a saying that if we give the Word of God first place, then God will always bless our life.

In Acts 4:12, the Bible says, "Neither is there salvation in any other: but there is none other name under Heaven given among men whereby we must be saved."

"But he answered and said it is written man shall not live by bread alone but by every word that proceedeth out of the mouth of God... Then the devil taketh him up into the holy city, and setting him on a pinnacle of the temple, and Jesus said unto him "it is written again, Thou I shalt not tempt the Lord thy God. Then said Jesus unto him get thee hence Satan: for it is written, Thou shalt worship the Lord thy God, and him only shalt thou serve"... From that time Jesus began to preach for the kingdom of heaven is at hand... And he said unto them "follow me and I will make you Fishers of Men." (Matt. 4:4–5, 7, 10, 17, 19)

Luke 4:18 says, "The spirit of the Lord is upon me, because he hath anointed me to preach the gospel to the poor; he hath sent me to heal the brokenhearted, to preach deliverance to the captive, and recovering sight to the blind, to set at liberty them that are bruised."

John 4:13–14 states, "Whosoever drinketh of this water shall thirst again. But whosoever drinketh of the water that I shall give him shall never thirst; but the water that I shall give shall him shall be in him a well of waters springing up into everlasting life."

Romans 4:20 (please read all chapter 4) says that Abraham "staggered not at the promise of God through unbelief; but was in faith, giving glory to God."

2 Corinthians 4:5–6, 17 says, "For we preach not ourselves your servant for Jesus CHRIST the Lord... "For God who commanded the LIGHT to shine out of darkness, hath "shine in our hearts to give the light... "For our light affliction which is but for a moment, working for us a far more exceeding and eternal weight of glory."

Ephesians 4:4–6 says, "There is one body, and one spirit, even as ye are called in one hope of your calling; One Lord one Faith one baptism. One God and Father of all, Who is above all and through all, and in you all."

Philippians 4:13 tells us, "I can do all things through Christ which strengtheneth me."

2 Timothy 4:17 says, "I have fought a good fight I have finished my course, I have kept the faith."

2 Timothy, 4 :17: 18 states, "The Lord stood with me and strengthened me; And the Lord Shall deliver me from every evil works and will preserve me unto his kingdom to be glory for ever and ever. Amen."

Hebrews 4:12 says, "For the Word of God is quick, and powerful, and sharper than any two edged sword."

James 4:7 tells us to "Submit yourselves therefore to God. Resist the devil, and the devil will flee from you. Draw night to God and God will draw nigh to you."

1 John 4:18–19 says, "There is no fear in Love; but perfect love casteth out fear because fear hath torment. He that feareth is not made perfect in Love. We love him because he first loved us."

3 John 2 tells us," Beloved, I wish above all things that thou mayest prosper and be in health, even as thy soul prospereth."

Psalm 23: The Lord is my shepherd I shall not want he maketh me lie down in Green Pastures he leads me beside the Still Water he restoreth my soul he leads me in the paths of righteousness for his name's sake yea though I walk through the valley of the shadow of death I will fear no evil for thou art with me thy rod and thy staff they comfort me. Thou preparest a table before me in the presence of my enemy He anointed my head with oil my cup runneth over for surely goodness and mercy shall follow me all the days of my life and I should dwell in the house of the Lord forever."

Psalm 91:10–11 assures us: "There shall no evil befall thee, neither shall any plague come nigh thy dwelling. For he shall give his angels over thee to keep thee in all thy ways."

Psalm 94:22 states, "But the Lord is my defence and my God is the rock of my refuge."

Proverbs 5:15 says, "Drink water out of thine own cistern and running waters out of thine own well."

2 Timothy 1:7 says, "For God has not given us a spirit of Fear but of power and love and a sound mind."

Exodus 19:5 says, "there is therefore if you will obey my voice indeed and keep my Covenant then you shall be a particular treasure Into Me Above All The People for all the Earth is mine (you must have a covenant relationship with Christ.

In Exodus 20, read the Ten Commandments. Verse 1 says we should have no other gods before God.

Deuteronomy 6:5 "and thou shalt love the Lord thy God with all thy heart with all thy soul and with all thy might."

John 14:15 says, "if you love me you keep my Commandments."

John 10: 27 My sheep hear my voice and I know them and they follow me.

John 11:4 "the sickness is not unto death but for the glory of God."

Matthew 22:37–38 says, "Thou shalt love the Lord thy God with all thy heart with all thy soul and with all thy mind this is the first and great commandment and the second is liking to it Thou shalt love thy neighbor as thyself."

Mark 9:23, states, "if thou canst believe all things are possible to him that believeth."

Mark 11:22 says to "have faith in God."

Mark 11:25 is the scripture on forgiving. Read it in your Bible.

Mark 12:23 states, "For very I say to you that whatsoever shall say unto this mountain be thou removed and be the cast into the sea and shall not doubt in his heart but shall believe that those things which he said shall come to pass."

Mark 16:16 says, "he that believeth and is baptized shall be saved but he that believeth not shall be damned."

Exodus 15:26 says, "I'm the one that heals you."

Psalms 103:2–4 says, "bless the Lord oh my soul and forget not all his benefits who heals all your diseases, who redeems your life from destruction."

Psalm 107:19–20 "He saved them out of their distress. He sent his word, and healed them, and delivers them."

Isaiah 53:5 assures us, "he was wounded for our transgressions and he was bruised for our iniquity and by his stripes we are healed."

Jeremiah 29:11 states, "I know the plans I have for you, 'declares the Lord, plans to prosper you and not harm you, 'plans to give you hope and a future.'"

This is my favorite scripture. Malachi 4:2 says, "To you who fear my name. The sun of righteousness shall rise with healing in his wings."

CHAPTER 1
The Beautiful Day

I'm having a sweet day. The wind is blowing, and the sun is peeping through the clouds that are beautiful in the sky. And then suddenly, the Sun bursts into a glorious brightness, and I feel the sun on my face and the life and the love from the heat pouring into me. I can hear the birds start singing, and the squirrels climb in the trees. There is life all around me.

I can feel the freshness of the wind rushing through, through our lives and through our own hair. We are thanking God that we have a beautiful day again. Going about our usual day, we are excited about what's getting ready to happen. Perhaps we will join up with friends who may be coming over today, or we may gather to go out and eat. We may just talk about going fishing or hunting or even events for our church. Or, it may be an ordinary day of going to the grocery store and paying our bills and everyday life of counseling with someone and telling them how wonderful God is and about His return. All I can think about is the brightness of His coming—our Lord Jesus Christ.

Often I think about our Lord and ask, "When are you really coming? Is it today?" I look up to the sky and ask him all the time "Are you coming today?" Could this be the day that our Lord Jesus Christ returns. The sun is so hot, and the wind is blowing so soft. The sky is finally crystal blue. Everyone is going about their day as usual; school classes are starting, and families are starting their day to go to work. The gym is open for everyone to go exercise, and the stores are bursting open for business, with money coming in for their families. Offices are open, lawyers are open, doctors are open, hospitals are open, and churches are open.

You could get your haircut and go get your nails done. You can find any items that you're looking for in the store. The shelves are stocked, and the meat department is full, and there is no rush to buy toilet paper. And you can think about spring that is almost here and also summer when everybody will be going to go hiking and on picnics. Mothers' day is coming soon. Teens are graduating from high schools.

How crowded this place is going to be in the next few weeks, with all the visitors attending at Cape Cod. Families are trying to find a great vacation spot to tour and having fun at all these beautiful Canal Lakes' beaches. I could almost hear the laughter with all the children canoeing. I was getting so excited about my grandchildren coming to visit me, knowing that winter is almost over. And the sun is coming out. It's time to do some traveling and so many more plans for the summer. We also have planned so many events for our churches and having camp meeting and families being there with their loved ones.

You can hear the sound of the train at the canal station, and you can see all the fast food stores open, like Dunkin Donuts to get coffee. Beautiful restaurants open that we love to eat at; life is going on every day as usual. It's a promise that we wake up each morning, saying the Lord's Prayer. And you and your loved ones every single day believe in God's Word.

With laughter and the air so fresh, you are enjoying the peace of God surrounding you. And the economy is doing wonderful. We can see the glory of God rising up all over the world. And everyone is giving praise and glory to the King of kings and the Lord of lords whose his name is Jesus.

Then, all of sudden, the newscast starts. Fox News is the station we always enjoy watching. I like to go to the other stations, but there's so much going on. Sometimes I really try?

Sean Hannity and the others explained a disease has broken out in China. Thousands are dying; on television, you can see those people's sweet faces in China. We see they were so sad, wearing masks in which they could hardly breathe through. So, we started praying for them in China. I thought China's a long way off across the world. I do not believe that it will come to America. I was believing that it would not.

Then I'm thinking of what caused this poison disease to be spread in their own beautiful country. What poison center or what scientist would do this to them? What really happened? You could see the fear on their faces, and then all the sudden you hear hundreds of people are dying. Oh my God!

Then you can see America going on with everyday life not realizing the seriousness of this. Then our president came on this TV station to tell us that he needs to shut down the airlines to prevent anyone coming in from that country to us. He said, "We're trying to move fast to save our own people lives in America."

Our mouths dropped open, as we prayed, "Dear God, help us." We started applying the blood of Jesus, and we started saying Psalm 91:10:11" Then we started talking to our families and friends about what we have heard, not realizing the seriousness of this and even in just a few days or few weeks, we would be seriously sick ourselves.

We did not know this disease was rapidly coming in to take our lives and try to kill our lungs and affect our breathing. It was called the coronavirus (COVID-19). I cannot even say the word, much less pronounce it. What I'm telling you is the truth and what we heard and saw. I let everyone know what we were doing at the time before the virus came and we got sick.

Then we heard Sean Hannity and the others talk about how serious this deadly disease was again. We heard it every night. I had to turn the TV off; I could not stand it no more. I'm a chaplain, pastor, president, and founder of our ministry called Power in Prayer Worldwide Outreach Ministries, Christian Church. We're located at 181 main street Wareham, Massachusetts. We started this church eighteen months before, and this church was still a baby, growing into its own fullness. We did not know that in just a few weeks, our church would be shut down, and we would be fighting for our own lives. And what would happen to the our church?

People were wearing masks and gloves and trying to find Lysol or any disinfectant they could find to make sure that everything is clean. They also were making sure they had food and water in the house. We did not know how big this thing was going to get, and boy, did it get big! I worked every day of my life for the ministry. We were trying to help the members of our church, not knowing the disease has already taken hold of America. Then we heard our president again. He said everyone must stay at home; the pandemic is really bad. Another thing he said was that we would have to be in a lockdown.

I know what lockdown means because I preached to the inmates in the prisons for seven years. Now our own lives were going in lockdown. I could hear the cries of the people who were scared, even in our own church. We were trying to hold on, trying to survive. We continued to make our home in Massachusetts because it was a very big move for us from Richmond, Virginia.

For years I'd been preaching to the congregation in our other church in Richmond, reminding them that something drastic was going to happen. Even under my big Gospel Tent that I preached each year in the prophetic, the Lord spoke to me and said He was going to "spank the world and America, and through this pandemic He would use this for his own glory to bring the church back to life. Will the church heed this, or would they continue staying asleep? Would the church keep having their other gods, or would the people repent and ask forgiveness and worship the Lord Jesus Christ.

When the Twin Towers fell in America, people were crying out to God and then were running to the churches. We thought the awakening was happening, but what happened? The world (and the church) went back to sleep in their own sinful world and their own gods. They forgot about Him again. How this must have really hurt him. I know it did. Repentance was in the air for a while, and then all of a sudden, it died. People forgot God again, and then many other serious storms came, along with floods and fires. Lots happened in the United States, but it still did not wake the people up.

Then they talked about killing babies in the womb up to the time that they're ready to be born and even delivery there babies out of the womb to reject what a shame. Some people in our government thought God should go away and get out of the way, but it's not going to happen! God lives in America too, and we're standing on His land that he created. Families do not even own the land that they had their houses on the Land belongs to the Lord Jesus Christ . *He* made the ground they walk on; He created it, and it really belongs to Him. He just allows you to be the caretaker of it.

I could hear the cries of the members of the church, saying, "What should we do?" To be honest with you, I was stunned. I've been preaching this for years, and now it's here. It was in our face before we realized what was really going on. God help us all. We had just moved here and were just starting a new church, dealing with new people, and we were trying to get a balance in the church. As every pastor has done, we dealt with so many situations and so many problems and so many sicknesses. We minister to street people and feed the homeless. We help our neighbors and consider them more important than our own selves.

And I could hear my church members say, "What should we do?" I told them to quickly get food stored up, get masks, and do what whatever you need to do. I'd been preaching for years something big was about to happen, but what the devil meant for disaster to harm, to kill, and steal and destroy, God is going to use for His glory!

The enemy thought he had this one. What the enemy meant for evil for the United States and this whole world, my God held up a standard against him. Church, the bride of Christ, you had better wake up and repent and get ready; the groom is about to come and get us. We had better wake up and get ready and repent because of something bigger is about to happen in America!

God was shaking the *nations* and was still saying, "I am still God. You want to serve other gods? I'll show you." God knows everything that goes on. The devil can't hide anything he does. God already knows about it because he has to ask His permission. Do you remember in the book of Job in the Bible when Satan was standing in line to go to the presence of the Lord? It was the Lord that gave Satan permission to bedevil Job.

What did Job do through the storm? He stood still and said, "Though God slay me, yet will I still serve him" (Job 13:15 . Job passed the test, and God gave him ten times more than he had.

God allows everything to happen for His glory, so now that you're in lockdown, will you pray? Okay, I do believe we do have an awakening that is happening now. We have seen all over the world that there are cries of millions and millions of people praying to the Lord. And millions are now crying out to God in their own countries and repenting all over the streets and their homes. The Bible says when the nation forgets God, that nation shall be turned into hell, but when you bow down and pray and repent, God will heal that land.

Thousands and thousands are repenting; that's what I'm seeing. Through this lockdown I'm seeing that people and families are back together; they're starting to love one another, and they're starting to come back to one another and forgive. Families and friends are starting to listen to one another. Through this pandemic, they're saying our nation is built under God, one nation under God.

President George Washington spoke that we need God in our lives, and so did President Reagan. Also the pilgrims that came 400 years ago at the Plymouth Rock in Massachusetts and also in Virginia Beach were warning us about how to live holy before the God of Abraham Isaac and Jacob. They build a forefather's monument in Plymouth, Massachusetts, that did warn us what to do if we lost our way. The forefathers hid the monument, but how did they hide this big monument? I have no clue how big it was. When I saw it I was so amazed. Our forefathers taught us what to do to if we lost our way and we needed to find our way back to God. We thank God for brother Kirk Cameron who came in and showed us the monument. I brought one of his movies and showed it in our church in Richmond, Virginia. But now that I live here in Massachusetts, I actually can see it and touch it.

How the forefathers would tell us how to get back to God is unbelievable. When I used to travel to Massachusetts to preach the gospel in my Tent Revival and tell them about the forefathers' monument, they did not know it even existed. I would laugh at them and say, "For real? You've been living here for forty or fifty years, and you didn't even know it was here? They said no.

I drove some to Plymouth and showed them the monument; they had lived in Massachusetts all their lives and never knew that it was there. You can see her pointing to the heavens to reach our Lord Jesus Christ, and the pilgrims just called on Him.

Our Lord Jesus Christ came from heaven and died on the cross on an old rugged Cross, and He rose on that third day 2,000 years ago. And He lives forevermore. We celebrate Passover and Resurrection Sunday, which we call Easter Sunday. We had already planned a sunrise service, with a live drama ready to go. We had arranged our glass displays indoors and our live drama outside, depicting the crucifixion, carrying the cross of Jesus and showing his Resurrection. It was really beautiful, and we were so excited. We also had special nights of fasting and praying in our church. We were going on, just like everybody else. We had planned lots of things in church and lots of fun for the children. And then the pandemic hit, and everything was suddenly stopped.

But we still had the glory of God in our own personal homes. We still had Easter Resurrection Passover and we were still praising God, just like we were in our own church, except all alone with just our own personal lives.

It was good to know that we could see your own family by video chat. It was wonderful to see them smiling. We just had a new grandbaby, named Olivia, and she was playing with her new Easter basket I sent her, pulling her little stuffed animals out of her basket. It was so amazing to watch her. The hardest part in my life was her, and that she was growing up so fast without face-to-face connection. I did not want her not to forget me.

We did not let this stop us from worshipping God out of the church building because that's just a building in Wareham; we are the temple of the Holy Ghost, and we are praising him anyway.

CHAPTER 2

Tell Us What To Do

I could hear the questions in the concerns of the members of the church in Massachusetts: "Pastor Sara, what do we do?" First of all they were scared, they were concerned, although it had not hit in America yet, only just a few cases. The concerns was real and so strong already. I heard some members say they were not coming to church any more until this pandemic is over. They felt like they did not need to attend. I really listened to their concern of maybe this could be bigger than we think.

My concern was what we were going to do as a group of members, even though we do believe in the power of the almighty God, but we have to also listen to the government as well. Immediately, several requested by phone to have special counseling with some individuals and some small groups. I was also getting phone calls from many others in different states to help them and pray. I would reply, "Get yourself some food and some water." We talked about getting beans and peas, all the extras vegetables and dry goods like powdered milk.

I remember Lois coming to me and saying, "Pastor Sara, they are saying that we are not able to get very many groceries in the stores." Everyone had a different concerns about their families' health and lives and whether they should continue attending church. First of all I told them all to get food stored up and to get water. Get as much dry goods as you possibly can, and get meats in their freezers. Buy all disinfectants like Lysol and—anything that you possibly can to clean your bathrooms and your homes. You are going to need masks and gloves. Every individual must make the decision for themselves whether or not they should come to church. They would reply, "We don't know if we should be able to come back to church no more because we have medical conditions and different things," and I said, "I truly understand that."

Every individual and every family must make that decision for what they need in their own lives, and we will support everyone highly. We support you in your decision, and we are here to love you, to help and minister to you, and to help you in any way we possibly can. If you feel like you need to stay in, please stay in. But until it gets strong, I'm going to continue hold church services for those who want to have church and prayer. We continue in prayer with only five people coming to the church, or maybe eight. After that, we closed our doors to go into livestream on Sunday morning into their homes. I went to the store, and I picked up a lot of supplies, I did not know how many members or someone on the street would be hungry and in need for food.

I noticed in the stores that the shelves started emptying very quickly. The stores were packed with people trying to get stuff. I'm thinking, *How in the world can we find any masks*? We was not prepared for ourselves because we were trying to get prepared for other people. I did walk into a hardware store, and there were five masks sitting there, and I bought all of them so that if some of our members would need a mask, then I will be able to distribute them. I wanted the work of God to go on, but we would have do it in a different way to keep his work God going. Suddenly we had to stop our services on Wednesdays and Mondays and had them on Sundays morning only by live stream. That was very hard for me. I came up here to preach the gospel and do God's work.

I wanted to help the people I knew they were scared worried and afraid. I was trying to comfort them the best way that I knew how. Honestly, I did not know the extent of how bad the storm was going to hit us in America. I do not think anybody, including pastors, did. It was a shock to us all, I'm sure.

I do know the Bible says life and death in the power of your own tongue. So we had to be very positive and encouraging, speaking Psalms 91:10 all the time. We also spoke Psalms 23 every day and kept speaking faith, as well as Malachi 3 :10. I was telling everyone to please get the supplies and—Lysol and—anything that you possibly can buy, including water; just hurry and do it.

I called my family, telling them to please get supplies. My son Billy already doing this, and my son in Ohio was getting his family ready with supplies. I was worried about my daughter in West Virginia and—did she have enough food to keep her and the children going? And did she have enough supplies for the pandemic. I spoke to my older son, and he said, "I just got enough supplies for my freezer and extra."

We were having people coming even to our own house, and they were crying about the pandemic. I was trying to assure them it was going to be okay and to please stay home and take care of your family. I kept reminding them Christ will protect the families I told them they should take care of their families; that's all that matters in life. Some of our members called to say they were still having to work on their jobs. Then all of a sudden, I noticed some of the members start having pneumonia. I told him we would be praying for them and fasting.

The one day we had an emergency phone call come in from one of our members. He said, "Pastor Sara, would you pray for me right now for me over the phone?" He was telling me how sick he was and how he was so worried about his family. He was concerned that his family needed help, and he would not be there to help them because he needed to go to the hospital. I started praying for him. I assured him right then not to worry about his family. Pastor Donnie and I would step in, and we will help with your family. We will be there for them 100 percent. It's okay; just go get yourself checked out at the hospital.

He kept thanking me, so I said, "Brother Ron, you do not need to thank us; we are just servants in the kingdom of God. We are here to serve and help. You do need to worried; just get to the hospital immediately. Let's see what's going on, and we will take care of your family." They admitted him in the hospital immediately. I could hear his precious wife so concerned, so I told her everything's going to be okay, and we're here to help you. That following Saturday, we were serving and helping as God would want us to. Brother Ron called from the hospital. He was so thankful that we helped his family, and I told him we love his family.

Then President Trump came on the news again, along with Vice President Mike Pence. They said for everyone to please stay home. I could not believe what we were hearing. I guess in the back of my mind I wondered: *What in the world is going to happen with this baby church, with no people, no church, and no finances? We just moved up here.* Then I had to hurry back and put my faith back into action and say, "Stop it, Sara. God's Word said he will never leave you or never forsake you. You are going to be fine. We're going to go through this with the kingdom of God directing our footsteps that are ordered by God. Thank you. Jesus."

It's hard for me except to stay home because I have always been working all the time. Then I got to thinking. *Well, I have needed to rest for a long time, and here it is.* Then I realized I could get on the phone to start ministering to everybody who needed more encouragement. Then the governor of Massachusetts said only ten can gather in the churches and sent us a card of instructions.

Before all the coronavirus news in the United States and the pandemic began, several of our members were not feeling well. That was prior to all the announcements, but they kept coming to church. We did not know to tell them not to come to church, but now we do. We did suggest not to shake anybody's hands. For some reason, that came all over me. I did not want to offend them, but I just felt like we were not supposed shake hands at that time. I wanted to protect the other members.

One of the members of the church had pneumonia, but they said they were feeling much better. I noticed my husband shaking their handout of courtesy that we do and show the love that we have for everyone. Immediately, I started stressing to the members: if you are sick please do not come to church. Please stay home and take care of yourself. Get yourself some good soup, some rest, and fellowship with your family. We gradually shut the church down on Sunday mornings too. That literally broke my heart, but we had no choice to protect the people!

I was getting a lot of work done while we were not open, and then we were also getting more rest. I was really thankful to God for that. I was actually working from home better. I started getting a lot more done. Something I had not realized, which is something we pastors forget, is about our need for some me time, and I was starting to be so thankful to the Lord for that.

Then I noticed one of those members that came over to my house, and she was not feeling well—and then I noticed my husband was not feeling well. I noticed this thing kept getting stronger and stronger through the announcements in the television, even with the church members, and it really surprised me. It was called the spirit of fear. Even though we preach the Word of God all the time that our God did not give us a spirit of fear but of power and of love and a sound mind, fear came. My job as a chaplain and also a pastor and evangelist was to love and help the people. We have to counter attack against the spirit of fear and unbelief, and that's what I had to start doing immediately through prayer.

God used me to talk to our members by texting and phone calls, encouraging them, preaching to them, and giving Bible scriptures to live by, not knowing in the next two weeks, ourselves would encounter the COVID-19 to the point of death. We was not prepared to hear the cries of our own people and people that we have ministered to in so many states crying out. They became overwhelming cries. We was not prepared to hear the news on TV with our president telling us that were in danger. We were not prepared with supplies and a lot of other things. But one thing we were prepared with was God's Word of faith and how God is real. Praise God!

One thing I tell you and show you now: we are prepared if this takes place again. If something bigger comes our way, praise God, we have a battlefield plan now. This is going to be a different in the church now! We are building a different strategy pamphlet of health safety. I'm putting it together quickly to protect the people always.

Sure, God told us in His Word to call the elders of the church to anoint them with oil and lay hands on the sick, and they shall recover. We will continue doing that but in a different way. We have to protect one another and even ourselves. Pastors, it is okay to protect ourselves.

I too want to see my grandchildren. I too want to see my family, and that means everything to me. When other people do not care about personal hygiene and do not care about themselves, we will still have to protect ourselves.

CHAPTER 3

The Spoken Word of God

In Matthew 17:14, Jesus said to them, "because of your unbelief for very I say to you if you have faith of a grain of mustard seed you should say to that mountain remove! To Yonder place and it shall be removed and nothing shall be impossible with you." This only comes through prayer and fasting.

I always read the King James version of the Bible, not translated. This is original Bible that is so worn out because I read it, trying to do the research on the mysteries of the kingdom of God inside the Word of God. I've worn out seven Bibles in my life to hear what the Lord is saying. When you pick up the Word of God, you just cannot get enough out of His Word.

Let me tell you something about the Word of God. It's alive. I do believe if I had not buried my face in the Word of God and got into the spoken Word of God, We would have not a revelation about the mystery of the DNA of God and how He lives in our own blood. He showed me how to use His Word by speaking His Word to get out of our sickness and diseases. I mean that literally, the Bible is alive. What I'm about to tell you is the truth, I've actually read the Bible, and Jesus Christ's face has appeared in a 3D out of His own Word. I saw his complete face. The first time I saw him, I jumped back, and I said, "Wow!"

Many times he has appeared before me through His own Word. Now I wave at Him and just smile and laugh. Some people think it's just a book, but it's not. The Word is so powerful—and actually Jesus lives in His own Word. Only believe. When you read the Word, you can actually see the Father, the Son, and the Holy Spirit there. You can actually see wisdom and grace. I have read the Bible many times, and the Lord wanted me to see something each time.

Once, suddenly, gold would appear beside the verses he wanted me to see. I would had to run and go get some tape quickly because I wanted to tape the gold, so it would not disappeared. I have taped it several many places in my Bible.

I tape where the gold would really appear, and it's still there. If I do not tape it quickly, it will disappear. My God wrote that we will walk on the streets of gold. I've seen gold and rubies. Wherever the gold would appear, I was here, watching what the Word was telling me—what he wanted me know. That is just so cool!

How many have Bibles in their home, and they're just stuck somewhere or they are just buried and covered with dust? Have you forgotten about it, not remembering the Bible is really alive? And it's sitting right in your house. Get it out and believe it. It's your past, your present, and your future. It's a lifeline and your road map to heaven. You need to keep your Bible open beside your bed and open in your car; do not let yourself go anywhere without your Bible. God may want you to read it.

Do not replace your Bible with your cell phone because your phone has an RFID chip in it. Try not to let the phone replace your Bible. When you read the Bible, actually healing would come out of His Word, putting this sweet anointing into your soul, mind, and spirit. You can read the spoken Word of God for yourself and be healed. You can speak the Word of God to others, and they can be healed. You can see the Holy Ghost teach you and guide you into all truth.

The spoken word of the Bible is so powerful that if people have open Bibles in their cars while they were driving, it could heal and continue flowing through the car through the anointing move of His Spirit. I have taken the Bible while I was preaching, and the Lord was saying, "Open the Bible and lay it on their chest or their back, *and* sickness and disease would leave."

I take my Bible everywhere I go. I was going through the airlines one day. I needed to go through TSA. They had to search my bag because they saw something bulky that was black. When they got to my Bible, they could not believe it. Now when I go to the airport, I just take it out all by myself, and they start saying, "Praise God, we've got the Bible in the airport." Call this old-fashioned all you want, but that old-fashioned Bible got me healed of the COVID-19 and my husband too. I like to take my Bible everywhere. I'm not ashamed of the Gospel.

But who knows if God would like to talk to me and show me something in His Word. I want to be ready for him. If God wants to talk to me then I need to stop and pull my car over and park and let him teach me through His Word. People need to share the Word of God with family members. We need to be seeking God daily, not just in and out and out and in. Do you know that really offends the Lord?

If we not allowed to lay hands on the people or touch the people like the government is saying, then we must learn to go in and use the spoken Word of God. Use your own voice and bring healing to the people from state-to-state nation-to-nation. The Bible said life and death in the power of your tongue (Prov.18:21 so speak the spoken Word of God and say, "Rise and be healed in the name of the Lord Jesus Christ." Use the spoken Word of God and be healed in Jesus's name. Used God's Word and tell the devil, "I am healed by the blood of the Lamb. No weapon formed against me shall prosper." You and the Word of God must connect; you and the Word of God must agree. When you're all alone, and no one's around, you must learn to use the spoken Word of God to be comforted, healed, and set free, agreeing with the Word of God. And the Word of God must agree with you. If any two can agree, God will be in the midst truly suddenly! Take life out of the Word of God and put it into your dead situation; that dead situation will become alive.

We have replaced the Word of God with so many books and so many other people's theories. Theology has changed His Word to their thinking and they have missed it. All alone, the Bible is there to help you. It was written by anointed men of God, and only those who are anointed by God are going to see what the Spirit is really saying to the church. And, what he is saying to the

17

church now is those who have an ear, let them hear what the Spirit is saying.

The Bible is saying Jesus is about to come. I do believe there's another big storm coming before the Great Tribulation. Is it another COVID-19? Bigger ? (I do not know.) And, I do believe we had better get ready for this big shaking—and the awakening! I believe there's a great harvest of souls coming into the kingdom of God like we have never ever seen before. It's going to be a great harvest for the kingdom of God before our Lord Jesus Christ returns. It's going to be the latter rain and the former rain Joel talked about, coming together, and it's going to be an explosion of the wave of the anointing. It will happen suddenly.

Thousands will be saved, and thousands will be healed, running to Church to learn God's Word and be set free from all sickness and diseases and all drugs and alcohol. This great move will not be man's move, for them to get the glory. This great explosion of his fire of his anointed will be from the King of kings and the Lord of lords. He will have leaders and apostles and teachers and prophets and evangelists: men and women and boys and girls whom He can trust to carry His work like the disciples of the days of old. They will not want no self-glory. They will announce Jesus and make sure He gets all the glory, like John the Baptist. And then the rapture is going to take place suddenly.

If you been praying for your family and your loved ones who are on drugs and alcohol, get ready; they're going to be waking up by the fire of the Holy Ghost, even in their beds and in their homes. You are going to see a difference in your husbands and your wives, adults and teenagers, boys and girls; do not give up on praying for them. It's about to happen soon! Just keep praising God. Speak the spoken Word of God over their lives now! Have faith because God is faithful, and only trust in what He can do and just—only believe.

Apply the blood of Jesus over your family every single day. Never forget to lay your hands on them and speak the blood of Jesus on them when they go to school or anywhere before they leave the house. Take authority over the enemy that's in your house through the spoken Word of God. I love the Word of God so much. I thank Him so much for allowing us to even touch the Bible. I love the Word of God so much. He's so real. Why don't you fall in love with Him, and let Him be real in your life? (See John 3:16.)

For years I've been anointing the land with oil where the Lord would send me. What type of oil did I get? I got olive oil out of the store. I put the oil bottles in my hands and kneel before the Lord, praying over the bottles and asking Jesus to honor it for His glory. Then I would anoint our property and my windows and my doors and my family's rooms. Then Jesus had me to go to many different states and anoint the land, declaring the land to come back to Him. I would also use the oil to anoint sick.

Jesus used me to anoint the people that came into my gospel tent revivals to pour the oil on their heads and to use it also in our churches. And we saw that when we poured the oil on top of their heads, it would ignite the fire inside of them, like an old oil lamp that was low on oil and the wick needed oil to kindle the fire to become a blaze. We've seen so many people healed and delivered through the spoken word and anointing them with oil.

I've been preaching in the Gospel Tent Revivals all my life with my dad Reverend Billy Watson and my own tent for twenty-seven years. I heard someone say there were no more tent revivals; well, we never stopped the tents.

CHAPTER 4

DNA OF FAITH

I am sure you have heard about the DNA of your blood and what type of blood you have, as well as what DNA is all about. But when you experience the DNA of faith like I had to when I was all alone in a bedroom in the hospital, fighting for my life, then you're wondering how I could reach God when I was so sick. I knew God was right there with me.

Then I realized as sick as I was, my God was flowing right through me. When you're gasping for breath, you do not think very much, but only thing I thought was a silent prayer: "Lord, I need to believe that I'm coming out of this, and so is my husband." I thought about nothing but just getting well and wishing this unbelievable coughing would stop so I could get off the oxygen.

That's when faith comes into reality. Whatever strength you have, you've got to move into action fast and fight with the faith with all your might and with all your strength. I could not think of yourself only; I had to think of my husband, deathly ill, on the fourth floor. I could not get out of the bed just to tell him I loved him so much or to just hold him one more time.

I looked at the ceiling. I know that my husband was in another floor that I could not reach, and then tears were dropping down my face. I remembered the scripture in Hebrews 11:6: "by faith it's impossible to please him but he that cometh to God *must believe*." Then I realize a plan comes in my heart quickly the scripture in

Hebrew 11:1: "Now faith is the substance of things hoped for the evidence of thing not seen"

You cannot see faith when you are too sick to think. How could I even believe it? Then something inside me happens that fights on my behalf before you even know it. And that is your real DNA, the Father of faith inside.

The Lord told me, "You have to forget about yourself now, Sara. Quit worrying if you might not see your family again just—stop it now! But you have to fight for your own husband and yourself now! Because the Bible says that without faith it's impossible to please him God." Through faith I had to take action with every strength I have left inside me And I had to take faith into action and move on His Words quickly or I was going to die

"The promise of the DNA of God inside through me will move every coronavirus out of me, and he will fight for your husband. But you must believe."

Remember God's Word; Jesus Christ is the only one who can move sickness and diseases. He did it two thousand years ago on the cross. The Bible said, Isaiah 53:5"But he was wounded for our transgressions he was bruised for our iniquities and the in the chastisement of our peace was upon him through his stripes we are healed." When Jesus came, he redeemed us through the blood of the Lamb on the cross, starting with stripes that we could be healed through Him. We have to learn to believe it; we have to have faith. "Whose report do we believe? We believe the report of the Lord" Isaiah 53:1 Before the foundation of the world, God knew he was going to have a family.

I do believe that God knew you and I before the world exists. I do believe that God formed you in your mother's womb, and He blessed and ordained you. You had been set aside for his glory! He has anointed you, and now He is going to choose you to move in this last day. He breathes in your breath of life so that the God of the true DNA inside you becomes life eternal. No sickness, no diseases, will stay because of His Word is inside your DNA. Psalm 91:10 :11 assures your protection because of His glory.

When I was a coronavirus victim, there was something so deep that this demon spirit was also carrying the spirit of death and fear to destroy my faith in God and to destroy my life suddenly. It made me lose almost all my self-awareness, even my own mind. I almost went into a delusion stage. While I was wrestling in the bed, tossing, I had to get my faith strongly and deeply in mind. I felt His everlasting love so much when it looked hopeless; then God spoke, and his sweet love told me to go down into your DNA and grab the faith of His glory. He said His blood has already healed me.

"I told you my Word that I will never leave you and I will never forsake you. I'm with you. Be not afraid for your husband, Sara. I will hold you, and I will come for you, and I have already made a way of escape."

I went down into the inner part of my soul: my mind and my body. I could see the true DNA of God inside of me. I could actually see this and feel the scriptures come alive in my life and experience it. It was amazing.

I could see His love that he put there from the foundation of the world. I could see the hope because His mercy endureth forever. When I was laying in the bed, I could see His blood that He shed wrapped all around me. I feel the wings of His glory telling me to breathe. All I could do was cry. I cried most of the day, thanking Him and praising Him. I could see in the spirit my blood would dance at His name. I could see how the blood was defeating the control they were having over everything that did not belong in my body. I could see, at the commandment of the Lord, the light of DNA of God inside me was so bright, rushing to obey the orders of the King of kings and the Lord of lords. At His spoken Word, nothing will stop Him. I felt His love so strong. I told the Lord a long time ago, saying, No darkness can stay around me or you because of his love and he wrapping you in his blood like a blanket around you the blood of Jesus Christ. Thank you Lord Jesus When God created man in His image, it was a creation for his glory. It was man who allowed darkness to come in. If you have a grain of mustard seed sized faith inside of you, remember that the Bible said you can move any mountain.. Don't forget if you're all alone in a situation that you're in, such as a dark cave of maybe sickness and diseases or cancer or whatever, you can go down into the true DNA of God inside of you if you believe and receive your healing.He is real; He's alive. His word is alive, so trust Him, remembering God is faithful. The number one key is, life and death are in the power of your own words. Hold onto your face and never let anyone take that from you. You speak life to yourself, you prophesy to yourself, and you command your body to come in alignment with the glory of God. And, God will honor His own Word.

CHAPTER 5

How Do You Go and Receive in Your DNA of Faith?

1. Repent; surrender your life to the Lord.
2. Study His Word.
3. Believe in His Word until it comes into action—and action comes into faith.
4. Be baptized in his name (Acts 2:38).
5. Forgive, forget, and let go.
6. Surround yourself by Lions
7. Life and death are in the power of your own tongue.
8. Only believe; all things are possible to them that believe.
9. Arise and be healed in the name of Jesus Christ.
10. Receive the Holy Ghost and fire.
11. Drink water out of your own cistern and your own running well (Prov. 5:15).

CHAPTER 6

Surround yourself by Lions

Wow—surrounding yourself with lions! I'm not talking about lions in the cage; I'm talking about lions. They roar, and the glory of God comes out of them. You will know them in the spirit, but they are in tune with God. They have a relationship with Christ, and their mouths are seasoned with the glory of the most high God. They walk by faith, not by they truly believe unconditionally. When they pray, you can feel the glory of God shaking the heavens. When they pray, you can see the atmosphere change. Their mouths will be the virtue of the living Word of God.

When I was at my weakest moment, you do not want anyone to talk anything else but faith because you're trying to breathe.

While trying to live, you're trying to keep your faith so strong in making sure that you stay in tune with God to receive your healing and also to receive your family—healing and my husband also said we both had to make sure that nothing distracting us .

You have to stay focused so we can walk in the glory of God, especially when you feel like you are reaching for a miracle for your husband and your own life like I did. Nothing else matters, knowing that God is right there with you at that time.

When you have people around you, who love you unconditionally and you know they walk with God in their life, that makes a big difference when the storm hits your family. The Bible says to "know them that labor among you." 1Thessalonians 5:12

When this sick disease of the coronavirus demon came in the USA and around my husband and I we had to be more alert at that time who we could let come near us or even talk with on the phone or by texting because one word of negative unbelief, doubt and prayerlessness could bring us into a whirlwind of sickness to death. Even though we were pastors in our own church, we still needed to lean on lions of faith to minister the Word of God over us in prayer and fasting.

We were excited, knowing that all the years we had been preaching the gospel to so many, they became lions to our lives. Thank God for the lions.

If you do not surround yourself by Lions in your life to put a wall up of protection around you, then you set yourself up for a disaster when someone else speaks death to you. Not only talking so much negative and so much doubt will brings so much sickening. They mostly speaking multiple offenses against you or your loved one. Then they start attacking you right when you are at your weakest moment, and you think, *Oh my God, who are these people?* If they speak one negative word or doubt, it can change the course of God healing for you or your family member. Beware!

Lions will be praying for you and seeking God for you and helping you think positive, even over the phone. If they cannot come and see you, they can still pray by phone. No one could come and see us because we were in the hospital; because of a pandemic, the hospital was locked down. Even in the privacy of our own home, we had to be very careful.

People want to know everything. They will question you and try to get answers from you, even when you're not feeling at your best, for their own personal needs gossip. They need to be praying for you until the answers come and then rejoice. We have a special associate pastor in our church whose name is Antoinette. She became a warrior and a lion for us and the church. I want to say thank you so much and for your love for support and for your prayers. She's very quiet, very reserved, and very much respected.

Calling me on the phone when I was laying in the bed at the hospital, she would say, "Hello, Pastor, can I pray for you today?" She never talked about junk and never talked about anything in the church; she always talked about God healing us. She would assure me not to worry about anything; the Lord had everything in control. She assured me that God would direct her about the church, everything will be all right, and not to worry.

Then she offered to pray for us. At a certain time each day, she would call me and minister to me—over the phone only in prayer, nothing else.

And the glory of God would come out of her like a lion, and I could feel the power of God coming through me while she prayed. She did not yell; she did not scream. It was so soft and so sweet, just exactly what I needed. She would minister in prayer, and after she ministered to me, I could go to sleep, feeling blessed. You need faith believers surrounding you. At that time, all the concerns about the church was in her hands, not mine anymore.

At that moment I passed the torch to her to carry on the work until we knew God's decision about us. He used her to keep everything in divine order for his kingdom.

There are certain lions who can help you get to your destiny. They are not out for self-glory or to control to take over; they are there only to be a blessing in your life or to be a blessing in your work you have upon this earth.

Saints who are lions stick together; they do not like to spend time with weak people. Weak people will break you down and try to crush you. Beware!

Learn to master your skills with God's help of discernment. You can tell a weak person because they are not really spiritual or in tune with God because that person is very unbalanced, always negative and judgmental about someone else. They hear someone gossip something that is not true and then draw their own conclusion, which could be very wrong. And then they confront you with the wrong conclusion to make you believe that you are wrong. They hear what they want to hear and then realize their mistake and say they're sorry! That's how you know that they are weak and not strong in the Lord. Surround yourself by lions who can help you heal quickly.

CHAPTER 7

Pastor Sara's Personal Testimony

I was shocked at the doctor's word that I tested positive. I've been tested positive Coronavirus wow! I've been working for the Lord all my life! I want to live right for God the best I could. I tried to live for Him in the best of my knowledge so that God would be pleased with me.

As a little girl always preached on the side of the streets, handing out tracts, telling people about Jesus Christ. When I had grown up, I married my partner for life (forty-eight years so far), Donnie Price, and we had three beautiful children: Donnie, Cindy, and Billy, as well as seven grandchildren. God had me do work in my dad's ministry for years, and then God birthed my own work called Power in Prayer Worldwide Outreach Ministries. God used me in many states and to start two churches. My husband and I have seen many people healed and set free and delivered. God even healed me with many miracles.

But I've never expect anything like this in my life such as we have experienced in coronavirus. But no one's ever prepared for something like this. You hear on the news coronavirus has hit America, and many have the disease. You've heard it has taken thousands of lives, and people are dying all over the world. And now you have this disease, and your husband has it also—and you just heard that two of your church members have this disease. It's almost more than you can bear.

And you speak those words from Isaiah 54: 17 no weapon formed against you shall prosper." Then you speak the Word of God from Isaiah 53:5: "But he was wounded for our transgressions he was bruised for our iniquities and the chastisement of our peace was upon him and with his stripes we are healed."

Psalm 91:10:11 says, "There shall evil befall thee neither should any plague come nigh thy dwelling For he shall give his Angel charge over thee,to keep thee in all thy ways."

Nothing in this world ever prepares us for what we faced. Then came the aftershock and knowing that God was keeping us in our right minds for a purpose in His divine plan. We have never heard of anything in our lives like this, though you hear of something like this in the Old Testament. But when it hit your own home, it's reality. Your faith has to be strong to come through this, or you will die.

And our faith was really tested. I said, "God, I do not want you to test us. I just want you to heal us." However, His plans are more powerful than my thoughts. Issiah 55:8-9 For my thoughts are not your thoughts, neither are your ways my ways, saith the Lord.

The Bible says Psalms 37:23 our footsteps are ordered by him.

No matter what we go through, what storm we go through, or what problem we go through, He's in the midst of our storm just like Shadrach, Meshach, and Abednego. He will bring you through the fire, and He will bring us out every time. We have to believe, and we have to have faith in the God DNA inside of us that assures us God is real.

We speak of God's Word that 2 Timothy 1:7 God did not give us a spirit of fear but of power, love, and a sound mind.

I woke up one morning, ready to start my day, changing beds and washing clothes as I always do, and then I realized something was different. I noticed that my husband Donnie had a cough, and he kept feeling a little weak. But it wasn't bad at the time, and we even decided that we wanted to move some furniture around. But, as we did that, I noticed he was a little bit out of breath. I asked him, "Would you like to go and get this checked out?" "No, I'll be alright," he said.

We were listening to the news on the television, and we were trying to continue preparing the church and our families and our own lives. We had made many decisions as president and founder of the ministry. And I had also, as a mother and a wife. I was trying to get everything in order as fast as we could and working overtime in many hours, day and night. I was trying to keep everything up quickly because this pandemic was moving so fast. Then I was going with everyday life, trying to help other people in my life, but I noticed I was feeling puny, with a little cough, I've always had a cough, but this was this different. It felt different, but I did not think much of it.

I was more concerned about my husband Donnie. I noticed that he just was not feeling good. He said he felt like he was taking pneumonia. Again, I told him it would be a good idea to go get it checked out, but he said he did not want to go and it was okay. I said I'd take care of him the best I could and I did. I fixed our meals as usual. Then I had to go to the stores, and I went to CVS Pharmacy to get him some medication. I was trying to get in more supplies to my house and also to have extra supplies for the church, helping with church members over the telephone and trying to get them to understand how God is with us through these tough times, and we were going to be okay.

We're all are in this together; we're going to fight together.

I had done every chore in the house that I had to get done, even making sure the vehicles have gas. I finished every piece of office work I was trying to get done.

That was before the news came on television with President Trump saying we are having a pandemic. There were no talks about coronavirus prior to that. We were on our way to Richmond, Virginia. Pastor Donnie decided he wanted to go back to West Virginia to do some work on our property we had there. We were packing our bags and getting excited. I was getting the house all cleaned up. I could not wait to pick up my youngest boy named BB. It's really my grandson, but the Lord let me raise him as a young child. I'm so thankful for him; he's like my right arm and strength. I love my BB who is really named Billy. Billy was in Richmond, Virginia, visiting his dad and his stepmother Tammy and his new baby sister Olivia.

Billy's father just got him a brand new car, and he was so excited about that, Billy had just turned sixteen and a half. They were all going to Florida in February to have a great time, and then I was supposed to come and pick him up and drive the new car back home. Donnie was so excited about going back to West Virginia, just to work on the land in the property for a couple months.

West Virginia is our original home. We lived in Beckley, West Virginia, and call it almost heaven. West Virginia is beautiful place. If you have never been to West Virginia, you need to go. I rented my husband a car in Richmond, Virginia, then he was going to drive up to West Virginia and have some fun. I was flying down to join him, and then we were going to pick up Billy and drive his new car home. We were packing the car, and I was making the house nice and clean before I left so I can come home to a real nice, clean house. It takes me about eighteen hours to drive from Richmond, Virginia, to Massachusetts. Of course, we would be staying one night in a motel, but I was excited.

And then all of a sudden, our whole world just changed. The suitcase is still in the overflow bedroom today in the same position. It had never been unpacked—I never finished packing our suitcases and it's been almost two months since that time because everything happened suddenly. I knew that Donnie started feeling bad then. I thought maybe he was just taking a cold. Then he started getting very cold, like he had the flu, but then he started coughing but not bad. We discussed that some of the members in the church had pneumonia. We thought maybe he picked it up from them?

Or it could have been from anywhere. We had no clue.

He would drive me to the stores, but he was really concerned about going on our trip because we heard of the pandemic. He started feeling really good, and I thought, *Well, praise God. Now I can catch a flight and still go home to West Virginia.* I just needed to pack a few more things, and everything would be ready. Then he noticed that the news was saying that it was really bad. Maybe if he had gone on to West Virginia, he would not have gotten so sick. West Virginia never had a bad outbreak of coronavirus.

About three days before the flight, he said, Sara , the Lord spoke to me and told me to stay here."

I asked, "Are you sure?

He said, "I do not want to leave you because it just does not look good on the news." Different people had called him to talk about it. And then I noticed fear on his face I do not believe he had fear at all from what he had been through. I do believe the other people were talking to him on his own phone, and I felt like the fear was coming through the phone to him. And I felt he got real scared. When he drove me to the store, he said I do not want to go into the store with you. I do not believe that I am supposed to be in there."

I said, "That's okay I'll go get the groceries. I got everything that we needed."

We started accepting that. He's not going to West Virginia, and everything has changed. I was relieved because I wanted him to be here just in case I needed to take care of him.

One weekend, we decided to help one of our members he had gotten really sick and was in need to help his family so he ask us.

Donnie went and help me that day and we had so much fun. Donnie and I were not feeling bad, but Donnie was feeling poorly. We truly enjoyed the ride that day. The sun was shining, and we were laughing.

Then we both went into Market Basket and two another stores, but then I noticed the look on Donnie's face. He said, "I wish I had not gone in there." When I asked why, he said he felt different. I do believe that we carried whatever was on our shoes into our own home. Even though I bought Lysol and all that disinfectant, it could have been on our clothes; we have no clue. We know our shoes are outside even today. Being pastors that we both are, as well as the evangelist that I am, we teach using the Bible at our Conferences. We both were not prepared what was about to happen. Three days later, I noticed that Donnie proceeded to get worse. One of the workers Lois came over to the house to fix us some food, and I noticed she wasn't feeling well either.

Thank you Lois for helping us and then I proceeded to tell her that she should just stay at her house until she starts feeling better until Donnie and you both of you started feeling better, not knowing that both of them would end up having COVID-19.

Donnie replied, "I could have just picked up something that affected my allergies from somewhere in the old house I was working at."

I said, "I hope you did not pick up the coronavirus. Let me call the doctor and at least just get tested. He still would not go; he wasn't that sick to really think that he needed it. Therefore, a week went by, and then Donnie never returned to church, and neither did Lois. They both locked themselves down in their houses.

I kept taking care of everything, praying and believing that they both were going to be better. I still had this very mild cough, with no fever or other symptoms. I've always had a cough ever since I was a little girl, so I never thought anything of it.

My grandson Isaac who called me Maw Maw, asked over the phone, "Are you okay? Do not be shaking anybody's hands. Please, Maw Maw, listen to me; you better not be hugging anybody."

"I said, "Okay, Isaac."

Then Billy would call me, saying, "Mom, stay away from everybody. I know how you are."

"That's okay. I'm standing on Psalm 91:10. Everything's going to be okay; do not worry." I thought, *Wow they are really worried*.

I kept taking care of Donnie, and I noticed he kept getting gradually worse, and then suddenly, it really got much worse about two weeks later. I repeatedly told him, "I think you need to go to the doctor."

"No, I do not feel like it. I'm going to be okay. I'm not that sick."

I said, Okay;

The sun came out so strong that day. I wanted to make sure I had ever thing done in the house. It felt really good to have me time. I was cleaning the vehicles and taking care of our dog Daisy; she is so sweet.

The spring was so hot but beautiful. I decided to change those mattresses out, but before I did, I just sat on the porch let the sun bake in my face. Oh, it felt so good. I noticed that my cough was stronger than usual. But I had to move those mattresses because I wanted to make sure. Donnie was comfortable. He kept complaining that his back was hurting on the other mattress. So I said, "Well, I have two twin mattresses downstairs, so let's get them upstairs and see if that will help your back. We started moving one of the twin mattresses upstairs, and we got the up the first flight, and I noticed Donnie was completely out of breath.

"Are you all right?"

"I can hardly breathe. I'm out of breath." Then he proceeded to tell me that he was overweight and he needed to get more exercise and suggested I sit in sun because it was very hot and it felt so good. I did not proceed to tell him that I was feeling bad. I did not want him to know it. So we both sat in the sun, and he was telling me how much the sun made him feel better and not sick. So we got that first mattress up on the top floor, and then he said, "I do not know if I could do that anymore."

That's not like my husband. He's a hard worker. Nothing stops him.

So I told him, "That's okay; I'll get the other one." But he forced himself to help me get the other one up, and it took everything he had. I told him to go back downstairs and rest. I would fix him some supper and then he'd be okay. I did not t know what was going on, but I just prayed. Donnie did have a prescription called in and it was a z-pack and he started taking it but was waiting on the dr to scheduled him into the clinic .They were over book or they were saying do not come to the office until you get really bad.

So I got the beds made for us to use that night, not knowing that in the next few days, we both would almost be at the point of death. Those next two days, I was scheduled to speak at our conference called Warriors Bride that met very Monday night at 7 p.m. No one knew we were ill at the time; we kept everything to ourselves. I called Paige, one of our workers, and spoke to her that we were both not feeling well. I had the Warrior Bride call in our bedroom. Donnie was in one bed, and I was sitting on a chaise lounge, but no one knew that. We both were not feeling well!

At the time we keep is quiet. But we kept the work of God going on, even in the prayers to build a defense wall around America. Then we prayed for our leaders that God had placed in our lives We had a long prayer that night. People from seven states came on the phone prayer line that night. I would mute the phone so no one could hear me cough. We both truly enjoyed it that night. Hearing everyone praying meant a lot to us.

I kept taking care of Donnie but he kept getting sicker. We did not know that we had the COVID-19, and I kept praying, "Lord, we need your help."

He was sick, and I started to getting sick, coughing and weak. I asked him again to please go to the doctor or emergency room saying I'd go get checked too. He was so stubborn; he would not go. I called Paige and Debbie, and Debbie just went through the pneumonia. I wanted to see what it was like, and she proceeded to tell me.

I got hold of Paige to come over again to the house. She is a physicians' assistant (PA) in the hospital. She went and got some more items from CVS, trying to help us. She also got some groceries in the house—food and extra liquids to drink. She worked so hard, trying to make sure that we had plenty of drinks they would leave at the door.

I then would call on our own associate pastor Antoinette and let her know what was going on. She would also bring food and help us. So also Dottie and Debbie and Sheila and we really do appreciate them. Thank you, sisters in God, you truly are the best.

God bless you all and many blessings to you.

Paige decided she wanted to help more, so she went to her job, and then she would come back to watch us and take care of us. I felt like I was coughing so hard I could not hardly breathe. I did not know I had double pneumonia. I did not know I had to Coronavirus either. I kept getting very cold, so I would turn the shower on as hot as I could stand it. I would get warm and then get myself dressed. And then I would start helping Donnie. I was coughing so hard. I would go downstairs to try to eat. I made me some oatmeal. Then I realized I could only take three bites, and I was forcing myself to do that.

I was trying to feed Donnie and make sure he was drinking a lot. Again I asked him whether he would go to the doctor and told him I was going to call the ambulance. He refused and said he would be all right. I looked at him and said, "Donnie, I cannot myself keep coming back downstairs to check on you. I need to rest. I was so tired myself now.

He told me later that he's kept watching me that he saw that I was getting weaker and weaker. I was so worried about him not getting enough to drink because I know that he would not think to do that by himself. He assured me that he would.

As I was coughing real hard, I had felt the wings of God wrap around me, cradling me. I felt the wings going back and forward, telling me to breathe. All of a sudden, I could hear the scripture in my mind and in my heart from Malachi 4:2 that say, "Those that fear my name arise with healing in his wings" and the scriptures that say, "No weapon formed against you shall prosper Isaiah 54:17 and "I will live and not die" (Psalms 91:10). I could feel the glory of God. I prayed so hard for my husband. One morning, I woke up my husband who spent the night downstairs. He felt like he could not breathe any better. I could hear him from upstairs; he had been coughing all night.

That morning when I got up, I was so exhausted by hearing him cough all night. I was so exhausted that I didn't have any more strength to come downstairs and check on him. I tried to, but I couldn't. I would yell at him to see if he was okay, and he answered that he was okay and that I should get some rest. I always told him, "I love you." The night had finally ended, and it was daytime, and I was so much in a hurry to get out of bed and see how he was doing. Our dog Daisy did something very different one night she always sleeps near the foot of my bed, but this time she would not leave his side, as though she was watching him for me. And I really do think her behavior said something was wrong, and he was not well.

As I got out the bed, I looked in the mirror, and I was shocked by what I just witnessed. I saw death all over me. I whispered, "Lord help, please Lord, help me!" I never said anything to Donnie, but I yelled, "Donnie, are you okay?"

I went to the bathroom and took a very hot shower. I got dressed really nice. I packed a bag for each of us and grabbed his Bible. I meant to grab my Bible also because I carried my Bible everywhere I go.

Then I went and checked on Donnie, and he was not doing well. I told him I just packed your bag, and we both are going to the hospital. He again refused, but I told him I was making this decision now. He was not breathing well. I told him I just saw death all over my face and that I could not eat or drink anymore. He finally said okay.

I called Paige to ask her to come over here quickly. When she walked in, she got so scared at what she just witnessed. I proceeded to tell her it was going to be okay, but when she arrived at the house, she called two ambulances, for the both of us. She did it quickly, and then I proceeded to tell her that I had both bags ready with our things to go to the hospital and they were near the door.

I proceeded to tell her of the things I would like to have done here if she had the time and if it were possible. "I'd really appreciate it if you could take care of her our dog Daisy and what we needed to be done." Then I handed her the keys to our home and showed her where the vehicle keys were. Then I asked her to call our children when we arrived at the hospital.

She said, "Pastor Sara, do not worry about anything. I'll take care of Daisy your dog. And I'll take care of the house, and I'll take care of everything." At that point I did not care or even heard what she was saying. I did not know if we was going to live or die; it was up to God now. My life and Donnie's life were in His hands.

When the ambulance driver came, I told him that they had to take my husband first. And they put him on the stretcher, and I was waving and crying out. I yelled, "I really love you, Donnie." he replied, "I love you too."

As I heard the first the ambulance driving away, my heart stop beating for a second, and I had a lump in my throat. I have been married to that man for forty-eight years. I was praying, "God, help us," in my breath. I look at Paige's face; she looked panicked and frightened. I said, "Paige, everything's going to be all right," and she replied, "I know it is, Pastor Sara."

As they put me on the cold stretcher, but they told me I could not take my coat. I have never been in an ambulance before in my whole life. I am sixty-three now. When they got me in the ambulance, they started taking all my vitals. I asked him to please give me an IV because I needed something to drink. I was so thirsty. And he did quickly. At that moment I never blamed God. I never questioned God. I just kept praising Him and thanking Him for His miracle He had for me. In my heart I knew He would in own timing!

When we arrived at the hospital, they told us we had to wait a little bit because they just took my husband and were putting him in a room. They proceeded to ask me whether I had the coronavirus. I said I didn't know!

They proceeded to ask me all kind of questions, and then it was my turn to go into the hospital. As they were talking me in the hospital, I look to the right of the room beside me, and there was Donnie. I start of waving at him told him quickly that I loved him. He did the same. He read my lips, and I read his lips.

I was so thankful that he was in the hospital. I was more tired on the inside of me than I could explain. I could not take care of him anymore, and I knew it. I was even pushing so hard to even tell him to please drink. I could not make him drink, but he had to do this on his own. Now I was relieved. I needed to get some help because I needed help now! I needed someone to take care of me. All these weeks, I had been taking care of him and others, and now I needed someone to take care of me.

When they put me in the emergency room, the nurse asked me, "Well, did you come and dress for me?" I dressed really nice. I just smiled. She did not know that I also am a registered chaplain and a pastor. Then I told her I was a chaplain and a pastor, and my husband was a pastor. The nurses all said "How nice."

I was so thirsty, the first thing they gave me was ice chips. Wow, that ice tasted amazing, so nice, so good, and so cold. Now I could find out what was going on with me also. The nurse was just wonderful; she was so caring and took very good care of me Then after a couple hours, the doctor went by just open my door. Witch was a glass door and did not come in and check me at all. And said your husband we are going to be =admitted, but we are sending you home because we think you have the coronavirus. And you are healthy enough to go home. But he never told me that I had double pneumonia. All I could think about was going back home alone in that room. I was so sick.

I asked, "Can you keep me just one night? I am very sick."

He said, "We can, but you will be put in the same floor as the coronavirus patients." He said, "Let me think about this," and with that, he walked away. He never checked me at all. I called Paige who said, "Oh no; he is not going release you." She called my daughter, and both of them told the doctor to please keep me. So he did decide to keep me, and they did put me on the worst floor, like he said, where the coronavirus patients were. The doctor never knew that I had coronavirus until four days later when the results came back He never told me that I even had pneumonia; he assumed that I had the virus.

When they got me in to my room, I was still so sick. The doctor came in and looked at me. Then he yelled at me, asking, "Where is your mask?" I proceeded to tell him I was told by the admitting nurse that this was my room, and I did not need to wear the mask anymore. He moved close to the wall and was scared.

I must have look very bad at that time. He left the room, but he never ordered me cough medicine or anything for twenty-four hours. The night shift came in and ordered me some cough medicine to help me. I kept praying to God as much as I could. I kept thinking about Donnie one floor above me. I wondered how he was doing, praying to the Lord to help him, and I was crying as his wife too. I longed to see him and just hold him one more time.

I could feel the wings of the love of the Lord in my room. I could feel the wings of His glory helping me to breathe that night. I knew when He held me that He had this in His control. I kept praising God that night. The next morning, a PA named Margie came in, and I told her that I did not want that doctor I had the day before anymore. She told me she would help me and ordered the medicine I needed. She said, "You look good to be so sick." I pointed to the heavens and told her that God was healing me. She smiled.

I noticed the doctor and nurses were scared to come in my room, but they did their job anyway.

I went into the hospital on Friday, but on Saturday morning, I was feeling better. The physical therapist came on Friday with a respirator to give me a treatment. She came on Saturday, too, and when she came on Sunday morning, she could not believe her eyes. She told me she was Catholic, and every day, she prays before she comes to work. She said, "When I came in your room, I saw Jesus Christ standing over you pulling death out of you." We both started praising God.

On Saturday Janet one the intercessory prayer warriors a that's in our church came by the hospital and bought Donnie and me a card and a stuffed animal. How she got the cards into a locked-down hospital was amazing to me—and that was a miracle in itself. I went to the window and saw her, but she could not see me, and then she started praying for us. She lay on the grass near the American flag. Janet prayed so hard as I was watching her.

Before she came to the hospital, the Lord was dealing with me to go down into my own self and into my own DNA, of him inside me and then into my own Living Water a well of his glory Revelations 22:17 And the Spirit and the bride says Come, and And let him that heareth say, Come. And let him that is athirst come. And whosoever will let him take the water of life freely. . I pushed myself out of the bed with my oxygen and then started praying and believing. I had to get my eyes off my own my own circumstances quickly.

And I started praying for all the patients who were in the hospital with sickness and all coronavirus patients to be healed in Jesus's name. I laid hands on both walls where other coronavirus patients were. Then I started praying for all doctors and nurses for God to give them enough strength to take care of these patients here. And then I started going back and forth in front of my window, repenting and seeking God.

Then I started to remember what our Founders Rev. H. Richard Hall and my Dad Rev Billy Watson would preach when they were preaching to us years ago. There was a day coming when you would be in the hospital, and some people would be healed all over. And I was reaching for that, for not just for myself but for everyone to be healed in Jesus Christ's name And I was commanding the devil to get off of my husband in Jesus's name. I was praising God so much, and I was glorifying His wonderful name. I was dancing back and forth in front of the window, and I knew that God had touched my life that day. And then, all of a sudden, there was Janet there on the outside, praying.

I was just rejoicing, then I raised my hand. When Janet saw my hand, then she started going to warfare intercession and prayer. I saw her taking the anointed oil that I have taught them to pour the oil and declare the land back to God. I saw her pouring the oil and dancing like David would dance. Then I looked at her, and she was on the ground in the grass, lying in the grass and praying so hard. I stayed at the window just five or ten more minutes, and then I felt a need to lie back down. She was taking over the prayer and doing the warfare. I went to rest again.

We came in agreement right then for God to move, not only just for us, but for God to move on the whole hospital. And then we started praying for the whole United States. I was lying in bed at that time. I got back up and looked at her. There was a man standing over her. She texted me that the man asked her what was she was doing. She told him she was praying for her pastors to be healed in the hospital. He left her alone, and she proceeded to tell me that she had stayed there for about one more hour. The security guard came back again and said he'd never seen anyone pray like that, and she replied that Jesus prayed like that. Then he left her alone. The peace of God came all over this place. I could still feel the peace of God that day and—the most wonderful feeling anybody could ever feel is the healing power of God all over. Thank you, Jesus.

My daughter Cindy Allen said, "Mom, I told the devil to get his hands off of your body. He has no access to your body." She was praying so hard. I called my son Billy and he was praying so hard. He said, "Mom, you're coming home." My family was praying very hard. That was such a comfort and a strength to me.

I got so hungry. I need some food. I realized I could eat, and I was starving. In the hospital, you can order your food every day, but you had to do it by yourself. At first, I got me some cream of wheat and some eggs. I order lots of ice and lots of juices. When the tray arrived for me to eat, it took me a little while to eat, but I was forcing myself to eat. I told myself I was coming out of this. The next day I ordered myself more food, then before I left the hospital, I had so much food coming in, the nurse come in and asked me whether I was going to eat all that, I said yes I am—all that and some more. She proceeded to tell me You know you do not act like a coronavirus patient. I said, "I am healed," and I proceeded to tell her that Jesus healed me. She said that's wonderful.

A wonderful nurse came in and told me to open up my window and get more fresh air, even though it was cold outside. I opened that window, and I let that beautiful, fresh air come in all day long, and it feel so good. It was refreshing to my lungs, and I was just breathing it in and out. Then I went to shut my window, and all sudden, that monster-sized blind that they had over my window fell down. I called them and told them. You did not see any nurses or doctors except when it was time to take blood or when they were supposed to come in and work on you. You were all alone, with the door shut. They did not want to come in unless they had to, and you could not go out. If you had to go to the bathroom, you had to do it on your own.

They came in only when they had to because they had to completely had dress up in a shield and gown and gloves, and they did not want to do that Early on there weren't enough shields, mask, gowns, and gloves to go around.. I was very patient, but certain things happened. Personal hygiene is a must for me, so I tried to get them to come in and clean my room. The cleaning lady would come to the door and barely went in my room. My floors was not cleaned for four days. On the day I was checking out of the hospital, a sweet little lady came in and saw how bad it was, and she said, "I'm going to clean your room. This is awful. Everything will be clean for you."

Another thing was that my bathroom really needed to be cleaned, especially my commode. And they would say they would get back to it, but they never did. I had to end up cleaning the bathroom and my room myself. When my blind fell down, a nurse finally came in and said they could not get anyone to come in your room; they were not allowed to. So she took an IV stand

and helped me. I worked with her, and we got the old blind up, so I can see outside. That was pretty funny at the time when the nurses and the doctors would walk in my room and ask what happened to my blind.

One nurse came in late at night and got real smart, saying to me, "Why did you tear your blind up? I tried to tell her I hadn't torn it up, but it had fallen down. I had to rebuke that spirit she came in with so I could sleep well. I did not let that nurse gets under my skin. I still rejoiced in my spirit. I would need tissues, and they would open up the door and throw a box at me.

By that time, I was ready to go home. I wanted to wash my hair so badly. I asked if I could at least take a shower. I had been sponge bathing myself before they came back in said I could not have a shower because there is no place for you to shower, and you cannot leave your room. I said okay but could I at least wash my hair? All the nurses was wonderful except maybe two or three. They felt like they were sticking their life out for everyone to be helped, even though this was their job and they were getting paid. I had to go into ever more prayer for them to be safe.

One evening as I was in my room by myself, I felt in my spirit the Holy Spirit let me know that something was going to happen. And I started praying. I called my young son Billy and said "I need you to pray right now for me. I feel like the enemy is going to try to come in to discourage me to flip me back into more sickness."

He started praying immediately, and then he talked to me for a while on Messenger so we could see each other. That was so nice.

Billy said, "Mom, everything is going be okay. I feel this now also." Billy and I felt the angel of the Lord camped around me. He kept saying to me that the blood of Jesus runs in our veins. All I can think about is looking up at the ceiling and knowing that Donnie is in some room, and I pray he's been taken very good care of. While I was praying to God, I asked Him, "Is this why You had me hear the prayer for the nurses and the patients? If that's why I'm supposed to be here, then I'm going to give You praise for it, and I'm going to do my job the best I can."

That evening, a nurse walked in, and she had a really bad spirit. When she walked in the room, I felt evil walking in with her.

She was very rude, making fun that I had ordered so much food, which I did not. It was just a normal turkey dinner with a piece of chocolate cake for dessert.

I asked for a cap to wash to wash my hair, and she told me she would bring one when she brought something else for me. That meant she was not coming back in the room. She said, "I have to put this in the microwave, and then you can wash your hair." I could tell she did not want to bring it to me. Five hours later, at about 10 p.m., she finally brought the shower cap for me to wash my hair in my bed, along with all my medicine; she was very late. I felt the shower cap she brought me, and it was ringing wet and cold. Here I was, sick in the bed with coronavirus and double pneumonia.

I decided I was not going to put this on my head at 10 p.m. at night, so I went and threw that thing in the trash. And the peace of God came back in the room.

She made it another smart remark that I did not look like I was sick. I saw that spirit behind her, making fun. When she left, I rebuked the spirit in Jesus's name.

The next morning, this really sweet nurse came in, looked at me, and said, "Good morning, Sara. You are going to have a great day because you're going home. This is a great day for you because so many do not go home, and you're going home today. You were only in the hospital for three nights and four days, and now you are going to be released. God has been good to you." I said Amen.

The doctor walked in, and to my surprise, she said, "Sara, you do have COVID-19 You also had double pneumonia, but there's no explanation how the DNA inside you was fighting against the COVID-19. You have a very strong immunity inside you that would not let the COVID-19 come near you."

I just about jumped out of bed and started shouting. She said, "What happened to you is very rare; the coronavirus could not come near your body. It tried, but it could not and died. You are totally immune to it. Now we need to use your blood plasma to help many others who have the coronavirus."

I replied, "Absolutely! I am truly willing to help in any way I can."

And then I looked up to the heavens while she was there, and I said that God is the reason why I am healed. She replied, saying she knew that was true, and then I said, "The DNA of God is inside my blood."

She proceeded to tell me that I would never get the Coronavirus again. She said I was ready to go home in about three hours, after your paperwork was completed. The doctor said, "Sara, for your age, I have never seen anybody as healthy as you. You are in excellent health."

I said, "Praise God."

Before she left the room, I asked her, "Can I ask you a question? Will you please check on my husband, and would you tell him that I love him so much?" She kept trying to assure me that he was going to be all right, but she could not tell me for sure because she did not know. She did reply that the same God who touched you can touch him. And then I asked her whether I could go see him since I've already had the coronavirus. She said she would have to go and ask to see if you can. She came back and said, "No, we cannot let you go up there to him. I still to this day do not know why! I did not understand why since I was already in the hospital, but they would not let me. When the other nurse came back, she brought me a real new, clean shower cap, and I washed my hair and changed my clothes so I could go home. I'm waited for Paige to come and pick me up.

While I was waiting for my time to be released from the hospital, I was giving God the glory and shouting in the room and thanking him for allowing me to go home. I thanked Him that I did not die, but He let me live. All I could do was praise him. I was not sick any more, although I did lose some weight. I was feeling so good, and all I wanted was something good and cold to drink and go home to enjoy my house, my Daisy, and my life again. I was thanking God for loving me so much.

Then Paige was able to come and pick me up. Then my next challenge was going to be even stronger, and that was my goal—trying to get my strength back even more.

All of us in our church started fighting for Donnie and Lois. I came home on Monday, and I had my Warrior Bride group make prayer calls at 7 p.m. in seven states. Everybody was on the phone at the same time, and they were praising God with me that I was home. I proceeded to tell them that we need to fight for Donnie and for Lois now and every person who has the coronavirus. I know what it's like, and I know what we need to do. We have to fight hard in prayer in the spirit for their lives and for America even more.

When I walked in the door and saw my precious little Daisy— was so happy she's a big dog—she jumped on me and she was so happy to see me. I could see the look on her face as we were being wheeled out in the ambulance that morning and the night before when she stood by Donnie's side and would not leave him. She had never done that before. She knew that he was extremely sick and did not want to leave him. When I got home, she came running to me. I'm so happy she kept giving me hugs. She's so sweet—our precious big dog Daisy.

My children and grandchildren were so excited that Mom came home. Everybody was praising God.

Paige picked me up from the hospital. She is the most amazing person I've ever met. Have you ever heard the old saying that a friend will lay down their life for you? While I was in the hospital, she disinfected my whole house before I returned. She wanted to make sure it was disinfected and clean before I walked in the door.

In addition, she said, "Pastor Sara, do you mind if I stay with you? I do not want to leave you here alone on your first night back home. You have nowhere else to go, and your family is so faraway to travel." I told her I could use the company right then. When you see your house again, it is a different feeling. It makes you appreciate what you have.

She made sure I had food in the house and plenty of drinks.

Paige is a PA in the tertiary care center where she works. She wanted to make sure my vitals were good, and she wanted to make sure I was strong enough to stay by myself. She helped me and Daisy in the house and made sure I was eating well and that I was getting plenty of rest and plenty of liquids.

My family became her family at that moment. All of my children were contacting her to see how we were doing. Paige was also chosen in our church about a year ago to be the Armor Bearer for our church as well. She has a proven her worth a million times above expectations and was excellent in serving in the church with God directing her. She knew that a lot of people would try to reach out to me and try to talk to me and ask too many questions when I arrived home, and she was there to help me.

I want to say, Thank you, Paige, for all that you have done for us. May God richly give you all the desires of your heart, including a beautiful husband who will be honored to have you as his wife and love you unconditionally and provide for you very well. Paige is a Christian godly woman that loves the Lord with all her heart and soul, with much wisdom and grace. We are praying for God to give her a husband of His choice, as well as children to be so blessed and that your life and everything that you touch will be prosperous.

Paige did not want to leave me because she knew that I would be here alone without all my family. She said the Lord told her to stay and help me. And I am so glad she did. No one else could come near me because I was quarantined for nine more days. She also did not want to tell me very much about Donnie; she wanted to spare me from being upset at that time. I really could not take hearing a whole lot of bad news after what I'd been through—the trauma of it and the shock of the storm.

You have to cope with all the emotions. When you experience aftershock feelings, you must take a deep breath, sometimes wondering whether you can breathe. When you go through the coronavirus, you lose your senses of smell and taste. I jumped at every moment, wondering if it was the hospital calling about Donnie. Did I have faith? Absolutely. I am a female, and that's what some females do. They can react, especially after the shock to my system with what I'd been through. Of course, even scientists say women are scatterbrained all over the place. Well that's true; we are all over the place because we are made divinely special by God. God did not tell us it was not going to hurt, but it does hurt. God said He would carry us through it. Amen.

Paige let me get settled in the house, then she and my family realized that it was time to tell me. We had a special visitor come to the house today. Our associate pastor Antoinette just wanted to see me; she stayed outside and looked at me and waved. She was shocked how good I looked. She said I looked amazing. She was always trying to help and pray; she is definitely a prayer warrior. Thank you, Jesus, for her. But she did not know that inside me I was just crying out to God now: "Lord, what about Donnie and Lois?" Antoinette brought food to my door, which was so sweet, and also four of our church members did too. And one brought flowers. How blessed we are to have them in our lives.

Paige had been having many conversations with our whole family. Then all the sudden, a super strength came to me. This time I needed to know what's going on. She Pagie proceeded to tell me that Pastor Donnie was not doing very well at all, saying, "It does not look good, Pastor Sara. He is fighting for his life!" I took a deep breath right then.

And I said, "Let's fight for him *now*! She Paige said, "The doctors are not giving him the right medication." I said, "Are you sure?" She said she was positive.

I stopped and listened to her quickly! When she started to tell me it shocked me. She proceeded to tell me that the doctor was not giving him the right medication, and he refused to. She started laying out what the doctor was saying and what he should have done the right way. I contacted Donnie quickly. He did pick up the phone, and I was assuring him, not letting him know anything because he could hardly breathe or talk—he barely could say hello! I spoke into his life immediately. "Donnie, the Lord has already healed you, and the Lord said you will be coming home." I took faith into action and decreed the devil to get off of him in Jesus's name.

I started praying for him. We could only talk but just a few seconds, and then he had to go off the phone; he was too weak and too tired. Every day I reminded him when I was able to talk to him that he did not have to say a word to me. I was so happy that he just picked up the phone. "I know you're not able to talk; it's okay, I love you, baby, just listen."

Every day I told him the Lord said he's coming home and is going to be healed. I constantly spoke faith into his ears. I reminded him how much we all loved him and to walk into the DNA of the blood of Jesus in his life. And then as we hung up the telephone, I always said, "I love you," and before he hung up, he would say it back to me: "I love you, too." He was too weak to talk, but I was able to hear his voice. I knew if I heard his voice, he was still with me. This was an amazing difficult time for me at that moment.

I just gotten out the hospital myself. Then we went to prayer, asking God for direction and guidance. We went to God to give us the answer we needed so much and how to fight this serious disease. We needed supernatural guidance, so the whole family joined me in prayer. We could not talk to anybody who was not a supernatural lion who could agree with us in prayer. Others' words and their lack of faith could destroy my husband at that moment. At that moment, I felt like I could only trust three people and my family, and that was it. I had people on the outside of the church in other states praying with me whom I knew could reach heaven with us.

Pagie e proceeded to tell me that what he was given was not the right medication, and then the doctor refused to give the right medication to him at all. She repeatedly told me, "I do not understand this doctor. Why is he doing this to Pastor Donnie? Why would he not listen to me when I've been in the hospital, dealing with COVID-19 patients myself, and we give them the best professional care?"

Was this doctor not educated enough? Did he not know what was going on?

So we proceeded to call every single day; even the nurses would tell us other patients were getting this medication, but they did not understand why the doctor would not give it to Donnie. The nurse let us know that Donnie was one of the worst cases they had in the hospital. I heard the nurse's voice myself say, "I do not understand it."

I said to myself, "Is he trying to kill my husband? Why won't he listen?" And I was begging for him to have this medicine.

My husband did have the coronavirus; he also had double pneumonia. That's what they said in the emergency room. They did not know if he had the coronavirus for days after being admitted into the hospital. The emergency room doctor told me he had double pneumonia; that's why they were putting him in the hospital. He also said Donnie might have coronavirus. I found out that doctor even stopped his medication for the antibiotic sooner than they should have for the pneumonia, knowing that he only had three days of the medication, and he should have had five to seven days of the meds.

I still would like to know why the doctor made that decision. Donnie would have been home so much sooner if he would have just given him the medicine. However, I do know this: when all else fails, even when the doctors fail, my God never fails, and my God made a way of escape for my husband.

Every day seem like a very big challenge. We had so many people calling us. I just got out of the hospital, and was trying to recuperate myself and figure out what in the world was going on. Every day, Paige and I were talking to the nurses and the doctor, trying to explain to him how it was important to put him on this medication and that it would really help him get better faster and to continue his antibiotics to get him better with his lungs. He kept saying they weren't using the medications Hydroxycholorquine and zinc. But this is what Pagie was using in her hospital, and it was working very well for the coronavirus patients.

We finally got him to listen, and he finally gave my husband this medication. You could hear the news media talk about how this medication was doing very well and how she had been using it in her patients. Then it was working for Donnie, but his doctor still refused to understand that this was working.

Donnie was also having congestive heart failure and also liver failure. We was just desperate, asking God to help us. Then in the next two or three days, the doctor finally understood and started him on the two meds we asked for. We didn't know if it was too late or what. And here I'm home, trying to deal with this and trying to deal with all the people at the church as well, and still was crying out to God while still in quarantine. I was determined I'm not going to lose Donnie. I told the devil he is a liar, and Donnie was going to live and not die. I had also been hearing that one of our other members Lois was very ill also I was trying to call her and encourage her as well. Then we had another members of our church was very ill also; now we were fighting for all of them for God to heal them too.

Everyday Paige would ask what his vitals were. She wanted to know everything. Then one day, the Dr. said he'd would give him the right medication to him. We started noticing everything was fine with his blood work. I was listening to his voice and heard that he was getting some better. We were praising God. And then the doctor did something very unprofessional. I noticed that the doctor and nurse just did not want to tell us anything that was going on, though we called once a day. But if we felt like we needed to how he was doing, so we called the nurses in the evening to hear what they would say. The family was on standby all the time. We could barely hear Donnie voice at this time he was so weak he was breathing and coughing so hard. The doctor still would not give antibiotics for the pneumonia. He was getting more and more weak. Once he started doing good, then he turned again. He been there for so many days. I asked him whether he was eating any food, but he wasn't even able to order his food, I told him he needed to ask the nurse to help him. He wasn't even able to order his food, so he did not get much, and he wasn't able to eat anyway. I kept telling him he had to fight. I would teach him over the phone how to order his food. I could hardly hear him talk at all. He was barely breathing and was coughing so hard. His lungs were filling up real bad and was almost at death's door.

We got to where we had to remind the nurses to please go to check on him and let us know how he doing, letting him know I love him. The Nurse so good they went and told him. One evening we got a very much of a surprise. The doctor finally called me. I asked, "Would you please let me see him by Facetime so I can see what he looks like." The doctor agreed. I was so excited; I was jumping up and down. I would get to see my husband.

I felt like if he could see my face, then he would know I'm still here pulling for him and praying for him. So when the doctor put him on FaceTime, it was Donnie on there. I was happy to see him.

For the first time in so many days, the nurse and the doctor made him sit up, telling him to talk to me. However, Donnie so sick. I did not know this until Donnie told me after he came home that both the doctor and the head nurse told him to tell us that he was okay and for us to back off. I saw my husband's eyes so scared and too sick to talk and barely breathing; his eyes was telling me he was so scared. His oxygen level was down to the low 80s, and his oxygen had to be on 5, and up to the highest it could go.

They let me see my husband, and I talked to him just for a few minutes for him to tell me and Paige to back off. I saw my husband. He was scared to death; his eyes was going back and forth. He did not know what was going on. And the doctor pulled him up out of bed to tell him to tell us not to be involved with his case. I am his wife, and I have the right to ask questions about his condition. "I just got out the hospital," I told the doctor, "and I'm going to know what's going on with my husband.' He pointed the FaceTime to himself in front of my husband and said, "You two back off now."

I was so shocked with this. Donnie was so scared; all he wanted to do was lay back down because he did not know if he was even going to make it. He finally got a new doctor that day. She called us to say he had been in there for ten days, and she assured us she was going to help him. She said my husband is in real bad shape. She seemed very and concerned and worried. I was crying and praising God that he finally had a doctor who really cared. All of a sudden, that morning around 3 a.m., my phone rang. I jumped out of bed. I thought, *Oh my God, it is the hospital.*

It was not the hospital, just a wrong number. But since we were awake, we decided to call the hospital to see how Donnie was doing. That nurse told us she had called the doctor to hurry and come to his room. But there was no response from him yet. We started begging her to call him again. And she did. He came to Donnie's room and immediately put Donnie into intensive care. He had no oxygen and was not breathing.

We were so happy that he was off that floor, and he was where someone could help him. I barely went back to sleep. I had to remind myself: *You have a family, and you need to rest. You just got out of the hospital, so you need to rest and let your own lungs get stronger. So you can be strong for your family and your grandbabies.*

I prayed and cried the rest of the night.

But my faith was strong that my God was going to move suddenly, and He would bring him out of this. I believed it with all of my heart. I was not going to take anything less. I was not going to let death have him now.

I started forcing myself to eat and drink again. I started feeling myself getting weak again. Now you can do this—you have to eat. While you're trying to cope with yourself and with your husband in the hospital at the same time, then you have stupid stuff come at your day and many distractions to discourage you, like texting. People did not understand the fire that I was enduring in my own home. We could not tell anyone what was going on because of their unbelief.

I had to deal with something every single day. I never got to rest when I came home from the hospital. Paige would have to remind me to go get some sleep because she said I looked very tired. I would listen to her and try to get some rest. Passover was coming, and I'd been waiting for Passover to come because I know when Passover comes, my God is coming, and He will bring Donnie out of this storm. Only God could do this because He was the Master this storm.

Because we apply the blood of Jesus every single day over our lives, our God is faithful.

They let me talk to Donny in intensive care, but he was so weak. God has blessed us with a great nurses. He came from North Carolina. He understood southern language and talked southern also. He reminded me how bad Donnie was, but he also reminded me how good he was coming around. He was also encouraging me every single day. He would not really tell me what was going on, but he was always positive and very encouraging to me. He said that he got transferred there from North Carolina to help with my husband, and I was so thankful to God.

Finally, we had someone to listen to us. Understand, I do know he was an angel sent from God.

The doctor called us, and I was so happy, finally, after days then a doctor called us. We did not have to ask them to call us. The doctor proceeded to tell me my husband was in really bad shape, and then he may have to go on a breathing machine. He proceeded to tell me that he did not know how he was breathing. He was very positive, and then he listened to Paige and myself of the conditions that we were concerned about the medication that he was not taking and other treatments. He was so impressed with Paige he wants to know more what she saw with his condition, and he took interest.

They went ahead and did another chest x-ray. The doctor could not believe what he was seeing. He said, "This man should not be around." He made sure he had everything that Donnie needed. The male nurse from North Carolina, I do not know who you are, but thank you, Jesus, for this man. He let me talk to Donnie.

I kept saying hold on, and Donnie said, "My anchor holds, Sara. Sara, would you please promise me you won't leave me in here."

I said, "I promise you are coming home; the Lord is going to bring you home next week."

He said, "I hope so,"

"No, I said, "there's no hope so you are coming home from; there is just wait and see."

Today is Passover; now we're waiting on the King Jesus to take over and see what's He is going to do. I was praying even harder to the Lord in a heart-to-heart talk, a personal prayer between just me and the Lord. I felt a sweet peace come over me. The Lord Jesus spoke to my son Billy, saying, "I'm not taking your dad. Your dad will be home by next week, and I will be healing him." Billy stood on the spoken word from God, and he did not waver, not one time, in his faith.

I blew the shofar outside; today is was Passover. The Lord's Word was coming to pass. I planted my seed of Exodus 23:20–25, and He said in His Word, "I will take sickness away." I was standing on His Word, and God's Word came to pass.

That evening we got a word from Donnie's sister's family that she had a heart attack and was rushed to the hospital. She loved the Lord so much, and she was eighty-eight years old. We all were praying for her a few hours later Donnie sister Virginia had pass away and went to be with the Lord we were sad and praying for her family.

In the next few chapters, my husband will give his testimony of what happened. To him in the hospital and with the Coronavirus.

This is when real faith steps in, when you have to be patient and wait on the Lord. "But those who wait on the Lord shall renew their strength they shall mount up as wings as an eagle" (Isa. 40:31).

I finally got to sleep, and then I realized morning was already here, thank God. I got no news from the hospital, which was good news for me. The doctor called us to say Donnie was doing very well; there was a major change on his condition for the better. On Monday, he was out of intensive care, and he was doing so much better. We were just rejoicing and praising God. I could not tell him over the phone that his sister passed away Saturday morning. I had to wait until four or five days after he got home when he was strong enough for me to tell him. When I did tell him, he said she was ready to go to heaven.

When they put him in his own private room on the third floor where I had been, and he had the same doctor, whose name is Margie who helped me when I was in the hospital and I was so excited about that. I could still hear him, still coughing and could not breath as well but he was stronger and t he was eating well, and he was up walking I was so excited, knowing that he was coming home soon.

Two or three times a day, I was talking to him on the phone and encouraging him, and he would remind me how much he loved me. He knew that he was coming home, and he and I kept talking about things we were going to be doing in Massachusetts and also in West Virginia.

I drove up to the hospital and said to him on the phone, "Just put your hand in that window, and I'm going to sit looking for your hand." Then he started telling me where he was located, and I found him. He could see me because I had my chaplain certificate on my car window. I could not see him, but he said he was waving at me. He kept saying, "I don't want to stay here; make sure I go home." I told him he's coming home this week. I kept waving at him and blowing him kisses, telling him how much I loved him in sign language. And then I had him on the phone, talking to him while he was waving at me, and he said it was so good that he could see me.

The next two days I did it again. I knew he was up there all alone, and he wanted to see me and was telling me that he didn't get to see anybody in there. They was in a real lockdown. I said, "Yeah, that's how they did me."

Something was wrong with his oxygen level that wouldn't stay normal. He didn't know why his oxygen drops down and they have to rush in to help him when he gets up and goes to the bathroom. I said, "Whatever you do, don't waver in your faith. It is going to be okay. God is still healing you."

The doctor contacted us every day and told me that they felt like Donnie needed to go to a rehabilitation center to help him learn to breathe and get the oxygen level up because he was in the hospital so many weeks. I said to absolutely do whatever you need to do. When they called to make the arrangements at the rehabilitation center, they told him that they would not take him because he was on the borderline of not being one of their candidates. I see that fear was trying to step into Donnie a little bit, and I said, "Donnie, stop it. God says He's bringing you home, and you will be healed. Remember, no weapon formed against you shall prosper."

On Monday, I told the doctor my husband will be home by Friday. She said that sounds good. On Friday, they called me and said they could not place my husband in a rehabilitation center, but we're going to release him or we could put him in a tent with the other coronavirus patients. I said, "Oh no; you're not; I'm picking him up, and he's coming home to be with me."

The doctor initially refused to let him have any oxygen at home, but then my husband finally spoke up and said, "I cannot go home without oxygen; my oxygen levels drop as you can see.

The doctor replied, "Mr. Price, you don't need it."

Donnie said, "When I go to the bathroom and my oxygen drops, I cannot breathe." Finally, the doctor understand this and started listen to him.

She ordered oxygen immediately for him to come home. His oxygen arrived at the house before he arrived, and I was so excited. I knew my baby was coming home.

Guy I told Donnie I would pick him up in the hospital, and I stopped at CVS Pharmacy to get his medicine. I got on my hands and knees to crawl into the back of the van to give him a kiss and hold him. And I said, "I gave you my promise I was bringing you home, and God was faithful."

I took a picture and video and showed our family quickly, and everybody was so happy. Everybody was clapping.

But no one prepared me for what I was going to see and what we would have to go through in the next few weeks to keep him stable. Paige moved into the house to help me, and I give God the glory for her. We noticed Paige was not feeling well, and her job ordered her to be tested we just found out Paige was positive. Her family was out of the country, and I told her to stay with us, and we would take care of you. So, we all took care of each other. She was a giant eagle lion, helping me with Donnie.

I did not care at that moment what challenge we had to face or we had to do. I knew right then the Lord let him live and answered my prayers. That's why I dedicated my book to Him because He deserves all the glory and praise thank you—our dear Lord Jesus Christ.

God was so faithful to our whole church and our lives and our families. No one in our church ever passed away from the Coronavirus but there was so many around the world that did and our prayers are with them all and there family. I will continue to pray for them that are in the hospital still trying to recover.

But I realized if you can go into the DNA of God and believe in Him, He makes everything possible, and he makes everything happen because He really loves us. Jesus not only let Donnie myself and Paige live, but he also let Lois live from the covid-19. And He also let two more brothers in the church live, who were very ill and —maybe not with the coronavirus but other sicknesses. Not one person in our church passed away because we stood all stood on the spoken Word of God. He is real, and He is so faithful to His own Word.

Always remember, God did not give us a spirit of fear but of power and love and a sound mind. I'm looking at my husband today, one month later. I wake up every morning, give him a big kiss, and I tell him God was faithful because He let me keep my husband. And we start praising God. My husband is doing so well; he works in the yard and does the things on the sweet honey-do list I have for him.

He enjoys talking to his children on FaceTime and enjoys the Sun and the fresh air. He thanks God that he can even swallow and breathe on his own and is not coughing anymore. He can hear the birds singing, and he loves to go look at the canal and see the water of the glory of God. And I point up to the heavens and say, "Donnie, it's all because of Jesus."

I was so thankful to have my husband here on Mother's Day; it was such a joy. We are the survivors of the coronavirus. To God be the glory!

CHAPTER 8

No One to Hold Me but You, Lord.

It was 3 a.m. in the middle of the night, and I was watching my husband taking his breathing treatment, and then resting. His oxygen level was back up, and I was looking at the clock and feeling my life drifting. I was so very tired and just wanted to get a good night's sleep. Every night since he came home, I've had to do continuous twenty-four-hour care. I broke down and cried. Who's going to help me through this? I just checked my heart rate, which was very low while I was having my own chest pains. Then I wept and cried and prayed before the Lord, saying, "Will you hold me tonight? I have had no one to hold me through the whole storm but my Lord. Truly, only Jesus Christ held me and to strengthened me in these tough times.

I'm looked at my husband Donnie in the bed, and I had to just cry and pray he's real good now, but who's going to fix me through this brokenness I felt inside of me? Jesus Christ held me to strengthen me in this rough time, through this brokenness. His anointing made me strong when I saw Donnie gasp in pain while breathing. Every time, I had to pull myself together. I had to be strong to help him fight to breathe; that become my inner strength of living well, even while fighting my own breathing and cough. All mothers and very loving wives always put themselves aside, no matter how they feel, to help their loved ones to be healed and to be saved. That's who we are.

Every night, I wished Donnie could have held me. I had no husband to hold me while I was sick in the hospital. I had no one to hold me, even while I was sick in my own home with pneumonia or going through COVID-19. I know the love of Jesus was holding me.

Having been married to someone for forty-eight years, you want them to hold you and comfort you in the time of need. And I did not have that or someone to say I was you're sick, "I'm praying for you today" or even kiss me. I tell you everything's going to be okay. I cannot wait to hear him tell me those words. Jesus is faithful. When Donnie could not hold me, then God became my true husband when tears fell down my face in prayer as I was praying for Donnie and myself. Then to my surprise, the peace of God came in His sweet love. He brought so much peace, so much love; when He came in and cared for us.

How many times I was up all night long, making sure he could breathe, hugging him and telling him everything was going to be okay. Then I would have to get myself up out of bed and be ready for the next livestream service. I had to be strong for everyone to say that this is who I am. God would always give me supernatural strength to do these things, and I praise God every day for it. I can't wait for the day for my husband to reach out and hold me. I would always kiss him and hold him. I knew when he was getting better because he reached out for me and said, "Just let me hold you." Praise God.

CHAPTER 9

Personal Hygiene Is a Must

E ven while you're sick or even while you're coming out of the hospital or getting better, it's a very must that you do personal hygiene every day. Some people just jump up and get ready and do not have time for God, but you need to stop and make time for God, and you need to take time have a fresh shower and make sure your nails are clean and your hair is fixed.

When we had the COVID-19, we made sure that we had different toothbrushes to use every couple of days. When you have been out, house come back home and gargle with Listerine every single day. The disease COVID-19 is nothing to play with; you must be a defensive wall against it, pneumonia, or flu. Please change your clothes every single day and wash them. You do not know the germs that you brought in through your front door. You might be carrying the virus from the stores or your job or somewhere, even walking. Always leave your shoes outside and have slippers to put on when you walk into the house because I do believe that I may have picked up the virus when I went to Walmart or another grocery store that was crowded. You do not know who has that coronavirus, the flu, or pneumonia in public places.

And it's important to leave your shoes outside because we felt like we may have walked the virus in the house. Now our shoes are outside, and we spray them with Lysol. When we walk into the house, we spray the area that we walked in quickly with Lysol, and if we feel like there's something on our clothes, we change the clothes quickly. We do not get scared, but we listen to our senses—what the Lord has given us and let Him help.

People might think that's crazy, but I change my clothes every day and my bed every other day. I change the beds every day if we're sick to keep the germs down. Remember the words that—life and death are in the power of your tongue. What you speak, you will have happen; if you speak life, then God will continue to be use you that way. Then life is inside you, and you can get out of the sickness quickly.

It's not easy. Believe me; it's very hard, especially if you have someone that is very ill.

Have your families to be really careful. Let children play and be patient with them. Let them come in and say, "Let's have fun during bath time. Don't yell at them—understand it's difficult on them, with what's going on with in the house.

Always please get plenty of rest, no matter what you feel like. Even if you feel great, keep getting rest. Take time to get the rest you need to restore your own self; sleeping is the best way that God has to put in your DNA to fix the whole body. Sleep restores everything.

If you have the COVID-19 or any sickness or disease, please disinfect your whole house, even if you haven't got coronavirus that I had. I had an angel, named Paige, who came in and disinfected my whole house. She was so good to help me before I came home from the hospital. That work was very hard.

I had a pretty large house at that time, and it took her a long time to do this. She knew how to clean everything and disinfect the house, and I am so thankful for Paige for the Lord using her to come into my house. It was so fresh, and after I left the hospital, she was just amazing. When I got my strength back, I started helping her to get her restored. We cleaned even more before my husband came home.

I set the table before Easter, believing he was going to come home by Easter, but that did not happen. I had set his plate and silverware, and put a large candle that glowed and had glitter in it on the table. I lit it every day because I was believing he was coming home.

When he got here, we could not bring his clothes into the house at all. We had to throw them outside for a while, and his shoes had to stay outside. They made him leave the hospital without wearing any shoes. When it was time to clean his shoes from hospital and his clothes I had to disinfect everything. I made sure to wear a face mask and disinfected gloves. I did not want to bring anything equipment from the hospital; I left it there. We didn't need it, as we had our own stuff.

When Donnie came home, he look like a bear. he had so much hair because the hospitals never took time to shave him. They couldn't because of the coronavirus, so when he was able, I got him all cleaned up and shaved. He looks very handsome right now; he was so happy to have a haircut.

Do not forget to change your socks every day. If you do not have a lot of socks, then just wash them every night if you can.

Remember, there is soap and water or just steam and hot water will do. Take a note of this, please; do not let no one come in your house who is sick. People will try to come to your home just to see you; absolutely do not let them in. Make them stay outside. Let in only people you can really trust, who are not sick; t you make sure that they do not get sick as well.

Also make sure that your vehicle is disinfected. I had to come home and disinfect both of our vehicles.

Remember, there is nowhere to vacuum your car and no car wash is open when the pandemic causes the government to shut everything down. Remember to always have plenty of Lysol, hand sanitizer, and lots of gloves and masks because when you get back in your vehicle, the germs that were on the outside of your mask is still out there.

When you get home from the hospital, toss all old food from your refrigerator. You can always restock when you get home. I'm talking about stuff that's open, not freezer stuff. Toss any medication that was open prior as well as anything that is opened, even bottled water. A pandemic might happen again, and we have to get ready for this, though I pray to God we never go through this again.

This is really serious. If you can sit in the Sun, that really does help kill the coronavirus and bacteria in the pneumonia flu. The doctor told me one time with my dad that you can actually walk the flu out of your body. They also say if you have sinus problems, it's very good to walk, and then I noticed that my dad would walk a lot, and if he would have sinus problems, then he got a little better.

Make sure your animals are scrubbed and cleaned and then stay indoors.

If it's warm enough, bring the fresh air into your house. Remember the sun brought healing to our bodies when we sat out in it. Remember to continue having the joy of the Lord as you go through any sickness or diseases or any pandemic. God is our strength, and the Holy Ghost will lead us and guide us.

If you are a pastor, then make sure your church been disinfected. The church needs to be in disinfected a lot, regardless of who and how many times you have services in a year. You should have your church disinfected. Remember to always keep extra supplies; you may need it down the road. Remember, we can do all things through Christ that strengthens us (Phil. 4:13).

Make sure you have plenty of water, I ran out of sterilized water, so I just boiled some water for twenty minutes.

CHAPTER 10

Be Prepared

B e prepared. Before we heard anything about the pandemic that was going on in China, we could have been prepared, having supplies and nonperishable stuff, as well as gloves, masks, and Lysol for the whole family. Now we need to be prepared if a second wave or another pandemic.

Have diapers, baby food—everything your children *would* need, and also please stock up on your medicine if you need to. Get things that you think you and your family would enjoy. Do not go overboard, but just get prepared in case we do have another pandemic. I do believe I've heard the Holy Ghost tell me that the Word of God is saying *this is just the beginning* (Matt. 24; 25).

Lay in *extra supplies* and certain things that you think you may need that you might not be able to get. Just get prepared and stay prepared this time.

Buy the equipment and personal stuff, and you will do fine. It may be wise to have extra cash, too—and tried to get out of debt.

Other things to consider stocking up on are makeup, hair supplies, communion cups (for church), and soap powder.

Make your list and get everything you need; always have extra supplies just in case this happens again. We sure pray that it does not.

CHAPTER 11

I Lost My Sense of Smell

I wanted to tell you how that I lost my smell and my taste. With the Coronavirus all of sudden you wake up and your taste and your smell is gone I did not notice it at first in the very beginning my husband every morning would go to McDonald's to get us a cup of coffee. He loved McDonald's coffee before breakfast sometimes we would drive down to the canal I look at the water if we hit the correct time we could see the train bridge coming down which is amazing to see the train go across that bridge and the water underneath and the birds swimming it's just beautiful when the train is done that monster Bridge goes back up into in the air.

We were not felt sick at all but I did feel different .I was thinking maybe I was over work with so many hours a week on my job. Starting a new Church is not easy but very challenge. So there was a different day he brought me the coffee I started fixing breakfast that morning I took one drink of it and it tasted so bad I took another drink and a hurry and spit it out.

I said to Donnie is your coffee bad and he said yes he said they gave us bad coffee. Should we just throw it away quickly not knowing it could have been the Coronavirus. Then we try to eat and I noticed my taste was different well I did not feel sick but just a little more tired as 2 or 3 days went by notice greater my taste in my smell was disappearing I put my favorite perfume on and I cannot smell it I thought well I do have a small cough thin I said Lord we're in your hands now and we do believed.

I am so thankful to be a grandmother and one of my grandsons lives in West Virginia his name is Isaac and he kept saying that something was wrong. Every time I was going through changes in my body then he would text or call me and say, are you okay then he was start lecturing me whatever you're doing do not you go to shaking people's hands. Please don't you go now were how could I tell him one of my grandchildren are all my children that I just lost my smell. I kept it to myself then all the sudden he text me said can you smell maw maw.

I just gasp for breath and froze Lord do I answer him or what?

I did not say nothing for a while then I said I better answer him. I said no I cannot smell or taste any thing he's just 16 years old. I did not want him to worry so I just start telling him quickly that Jesus Christ will take care of us and how can I tell him that I am getting weaker and I am coughing more than I should his grandpa is not doing too well either.

I wanted to speak life in this situation not death. Because the Bible said life and death in the power of the tongue. At this point I said which Master do I choose the coronavirus or the Word of God. I knew right then we had to start really living in the Word of God to come fully through this how can you tell your family.

It was not too long after that that the smell and The Taste was completely gone. I would try to eat something and you had to force yourself to eat because it was nothing taste good anymore I said that one of the first signs of receive the covid-19 diseases is to lose your taste and smell.

Now we know that to be true now I know that's to be true I know sometimes you have the strep throat or would probably have pneumonia that could possibly with your taste and smell as well do this but this will make a difference.

This smell has a charcoal bitter taste you could smell it in your nostrils down your lungs did not know what it was never smelled of nothing like this before.

And as your body gets weaker and tired you really do not care if you just want to rest.

It's still taking me a little while to get my taste and smell back.

When you smell the Easter fragments of the resurrection power of God's glory you are smelling life going through you or freshness of our air outside.

You get excited when even the little ants was birthing in to live outside on the sidewalk of springtime coming in.

And the Robins and the bluebirds and even the squirrels having fun everywhere outside.

You're so thankful to the Lord that he allowed you to live and breathe smell and taste again you definitely do not see it the same way you see it was fresh eyes of the glory of God and being thankful and repenting.

I do not know that when the storm comes he's right there to carry you through the storm because our anchor holds in Jesus.

CHAPTER 12

How Do I Tell My Family?

believe that was the hardest decision I had to make was to tell my own family. I prayed really hard, asking God what to tell them. This was not going to be easy, but I had to do it, so I just picked up the phone and told them I needed to talk to them. I talked to everyone individually. I think Isaac already knew. I believe the Lord was revealing to him that something was going to happen to us.

VISION FROM MY DAUGHTER

Cindy, my daughter, had a vision one night a few weeks prior to anything taking place in the nation, and she proceeded to tell me how she was fighting hard and running to get to us. But it was very difficult. When she arrived at the hospital, she heard from the doctors that her dad had already passed away. Then she went in my room also, and she was telling me, "Mom, you need to go down deep and fight and live. Your family needs you to live. Mom, please do not pass away." Then she started praying. I do believe that the Lord showed her that something powerful was getting ready to happen to her parents and that she needed to be alert, fasting and praying and seeking God.

As she proceeded to tell me, for a few minutes, I was just a little shocked, and after I got myself together, I told Cindy that was just a dream. But I suggested we pray that whatever the enemy meant for harm, God would to turn it to His glory. I was trying to ease her mind that nothing was going to happen to us and that we were under the hands of God, as in Psalms 91:10 and

Psalms 23 that says:

> The Lord is my Shepherd;" I shall not want. He maketh me lie down in green pastures: he leadeth me beside the Still water. He restoreth my soul: he leadeth me in the paths of righteousness for his name's sake. Yea, though I walk through the valley of the shadow of death, I will fear no evil for thou art with me; thy rod and staff it comfort me. Thou preparest a table before me in the presence of my enemies: thou anointest my head with oil; my cup runneth. over. Surely goodness and mercy shall follow me all the days of my life and I shall dwell in the house of the Lord forever.

After we got off the phone, it took me back just for a little bit. I asked my God what He was trying to tell Cindy because God is trying to warn us about something. So right then, we broke the dream in prayer and the division of the enemy that would try to tear us down. We commanded it to die at the name of Jesus Christ

I remember trying to assure her that everything was going to be all right, not knowing that in the next couple months, we would be fighting for our own life to live because of the COVID-19. What the enemy meant for harm, God turned it for His glory. While we were going through this storm, we both discuss the dream again—how God was warned her to be alert and be aware that something was going to happen to her parents and get prepared. When you're close to God, He will show you things that He needs you to know concerning people, places, and things to help them or to help yourself to be prepared. Well, a storm was coming. I'm sure she prayed, and I'm sure that stayed in the back of her mind.

I thank God for a beautiful, praying daughter that He have gave us. She looks just looks like her father. And I'm believing God for the best for her and for God to strengthen her all the days of her life. God is raising her up to be a prophetess, and God is going to use her in the last days because she has passed all the tests she has been through, and God is very pleased with her progress. The Lord has groomed her for His glory. And I know I'll get to see it in the fullness of the glory inside her. God is already blossoming and blooming in her life for His kingdom. Thank you, Jesus.

Cindy, Jesus loves you so much, and so do I.

How can we tell our children that we were very sick and we might have COVID-19 in a pandemic of a storm up here in Massachusetts as well as the world? We were hundreds of miles away, and we may never see each other again. I picked up the phone and started calling everyone individually.

I called my son Billy Paul Price first. I said, "Billy, I need to talk to you. Can we FaceTime? We did through this pandemic, he and his precious wife Tammy and their new baby Olivia. I was crying in the bed so sick. How was I going to tell them that I may never see Olivia again. I wanted her to know that her grandmother loved her so much. She's so beautiful. So while I was talking to him on the phone I said really need to tell you something. Your dad is not doing good, and it do not look good. We haven't been tested yet, but I do think we have the COVID-19 I do know he does have pneumonia. Not only is he not feeling well, but your mom's not feeling well either. And we need you to pray for both of us. Will you talked to God to help us in prayer."

I saw the expression on his face go from a smile to tears dropping down his face. He said, "Mom, I don't want to lose you and Dad." I had to go real deep right then.

I said, "You're not; I just need you to pray." I kept telling him it was going to be okay. I told him I needed to go and tell his son Billy, my grandson, that his maw maw's not doing too good, nor his paw paw.

We don't know what the outcome of this will be, but we know it's going to be the will of God. He has our lives in his hands, and whatever happens will be for His glory.

As tears dripped down both of our faces, I realized this is reality; this is real and—this is really happening to us. God, whether we live or we die, we are winners either way. Seeing the look on his face, I said, "God, help us please."

He got off the phone, and I believe he went to the park and prayed so hard. He did not give up until he heard from God that we were going to be okay. Every day he would FaceTime me and say, "Mom, the blood of Jesus runs in your veins." I saw God birth a new beginning of the glory of God inside him. I saw him preaching to me on the phone, and we started having Bible studies on the phone about Revelation. He picked up his grandpa Reverend Billy Watson's, book of Revelation that I gave him.

Then he said he was studying it backwards and forwards, and he kept his mind on the Word of God, believing that we're going to be okay. Billy is the one who told me that God told him that his dad was coming home and that everything was going to be okay. Billy stood on the spoken Word of God literally that everything was going to be okay, that God was going to heal us both and that we would see his family again.

That was such a comfort to my soul God added to my life that day No matter how I felt, I stayed on the phone with him every day as much as he could, and I could just to see his face, Olivia's face, and Billy's face.

He was walking out in the woods one time, and he said, "Come on, Mom, you walk with me, and I got to be with him walking through the woods on video chat while he was praying and talking to God. We were discussing lots of other things, and I got my mind off of my sickness and onto what he was talking about. He was letting me hear the sounds of the animals, and he walked and walked around, praying and talking to God. He was just literally letting me have a part of that day, and it just was so nice. I felt like I was outdoors with him. I thank God for the phone system. He says when he goes out in the woods, that's when he feels the peace of God.

My daughter-in-law Tammy is an amazing woman. She was always praying for me with her smile that she always wore on her face. That was such a comfort to me. I love her so much, and I truly thank God for her and how God is birthing in her a greatness of His glory to really shine.

Billy's family was always FaceTiming me. They let me see how big Olivia had gotten since the last time I saw her, and I thought how amazingly beautiful little Olivia is while she has her own personality. She is shining like a rose.

I'm so proud of you, Billy, the man of integrity of God you have become. I love you, Tammy and Olivia and BB.

When Donnie arrived home from the hospital, Billy and he have been talking contractor shop. It's amazing how God still heals today. My son Billy is an amazing contractor in Richmond, Virginia called—Price Builders. We are so proud of you.

I picked up the phone again and I started calling my oldest son, Donnie Price. He's a district manager for Pilot Sturbridge. I did not want to bother him because I know he had so much going on, trying to keep the truckers coming to the gas station and getting everything going in his own situation with this pandemic. This pandemic is just a mess, and many places are closed due to this COVID-19. And God blessed his stores to be open, and Donnie traveled so much, trying to keep everything running smoothly, knowing people at his job were also getting sick. He had to find people to work the jobs.

I cannot imagine how much pressure he had upon him. When I told him on the phone that we were very sick, and we could be infected with the virus, he stopped and took time to talk to me for a long time, and that was such a comfort for me.

He always assured me he loved me and was praying for us he would be checking on us a lot —and he did quite often. When he would get a free moment, he always picked up the phone and asked how I was feeling, letting me know I sounded better, and asking how his Dad was doing.

I would always assure him the good and the bad and that everything was going to be okay. Then he always reminded me he would come to see me when he could. That was such a wonderful comfort to me, knowing that. As soon as everything breaks with the pandemic coronavirus, I would be there.

Then I would often pray in my bed, "Please, Lord, take care of him and his family. He's had to deal with so many people." Donnie would assure me that everything was going to be okay on his side, and I said okay. He always ended with, "If you need anything, just please let me know."

I thank God for my son Donnie. I'm so proud of him. Not a day goes by that a mother doesn't think about her children and how see they are succeeding and how they have their own families. I am so very proud of you, Donnie, and your family Devon and Madison all of your success that you have built in life and the business man you have become. May the Lord bless you and his face to continue to shine upon you. I love you, my son and my grandchildren.

Then I picked up the telephone and call my sixteen-year-old grandson who is like my own son because he has lived with me since he was a little boy. His name is Billy Price II. I call him BB. He's almost six feet tall. His dad Billy and his other mother Tammy lives in Virginia. They have planned a trip in February to go to Florida and have an amazing vacation there. In 2 weeks we had plans to go and pick BB back up and fly home with JetBlue when we realized that we were not able to go back to Virginia to pick him back up Billy had live we me since he was a little boy. And he would not have been able to return home because of the pandemic. That was very hard for me to not see him and talk to him, but I was so thankful to God that he was not here and he was safe.

The coronavirus was so strong, and people were dying everywhere. I am so thankful that BB did not see what we were going through at that time of the Coronavirus—and he was not here through the process of us getting very ill. And I thank God he was not here to get sick also. Thank you, Jesus

I knew that would have been very scary for him, and he would also have had to be home alone at this house by himself and with Daisy our dog. And I am so thankful that God allowed him to be there at that appointed time.

His father Bill and Tammy I talked many times that God had everything and everyone's life planned for that time. His plans were made before we even knew that they were made, and then all of sudden, everything fit right into position, and we knew right then that our footsteps were ordered by God. We give him all the glory.

I'm so thankful that God placed him there in Virginia just for a little bit until he can return home. We miss him dearly, and we all cannot wait for him to return home.

When I told him that we had the coronavirus, I could see the tears in his eyes. He said, "Maw, we told you please do not get around anyone; please don't talk to anybody. Why did you not listen? I explained to him that we did, but somehow we picked it up and that we're going to be all right. He kept telling me that he loved me, and he would always check on me. He kept telling me that he knew that everything was going to be all right, that God had everything worked out. He definitely was not worried.

When I asked him to pray, he would pray—thank you, Jesus. After that, I noticed that he was very quiet and reserved. I do believe he had his days and nights mixed up and that he was a little bit depressed. He would tell me how hard this was on him, and he wanted to also come home. He loved being with his father, but he wanted to be with his own surroundings, his own stuff, and he was so thankful to his mom and dad for allowing him to stay there, but he really wanted to come home. He did not want to say too much; he was just very quiet and reserved. I can only imagine how very hard this storm was on him.

I kept reminding him that as soon as he wants to come home and felt in his heart that it is safe to return home due to the virus— and we have to make sure that it is safe to travel—I would contact JetBlue to get him a ticket and try to get him home quickly. But he felt like he needed to stay there just until this pandemic dies. He said he did not want to take that disease, and I said I surely understood that. So, we're waiting for this great reunion for everybody to come together cannot wait for that day. We have already planned so much, which really encourages us to pull harder to see our family. Because we are going to hug one another as a family. We lived and did not die, and we are the survivors of the coronavirus. Nothing is going to stop us from hugging our families because we believe that the blood of Jesus runs in our veins.

And we are not scared. We are going to have a rejoicing time. IT took five months for him to return home and he did.

I'm so proud of him and how God has made him the man of God that he is becoming. He's going to be a warrior and wonderful family man one day. May God bless him, and may God bless the footsteps He has ordered for his life. He'll never forget this year, 2020, and the pandemic that hit his family and how God rescued us all from the coronavirus. Hallelujah!

Now it was time to tell Isaac

Then I pick up the phone and called a special grandson of mine, Isaac, who he kept checking on me I had to tell him that I was not feeling well and that we may have the coronavirus. I assured him that we're going to make it, and everything's going to be fine because God is going to help us through this.

He was so amazing through this whole thing; he would call me every single day on FaceTime

He was encouraging me, though when I first told him, he was very upset. He kept saying, "Grandma, I told you not to go out. I knew something was going to happen. Why did you not listen to me?"

I told him, "Isaac, I'm a chaplain and a pastor. I have to go help people. That's our job.

"I know, Grandmother, but you cannot do these things. You've got to stay home."

And then his brother Luke came on the phone, and he was bawling and crying, saying, "So, Grandmother, is anything going to happen to Grandpa?"

I said, "I don't know. We have to pray." He cried so very hard.

The reality that really happened in our own home was too much for these children. To think that they could lose their grandparents was not fun. They always called me "the cool grandmother" because I did everything with them and we had so much fun when they came to Massachusetts they didn't want to go home. Isaac and Luke were not taking this very well. Luke is very attached to his grandpa, more than me, but he loves me. He's looks just like his grandpa, and he acts like Donnie.

Luke was waiting for Grandpa Donnie to come home and they were going to go fishing and different things, and Donnie had that plane ticket all ready to go to take Luke many places and do a lot of things. He was devastated when he knew that his grandpa was not coming in. Isaac is close to my heart; he loves me very much, and he wanted to come up this summer, but we know this is impossible this year because of the pandemic. I know it was really bothering him. My grandchildren normally come up every year to be with me; we have an amazing time.

Isaac would keep me on the phone, so I could just talk to him. Even when after I got out of the hospital, he kept me on the phone for hours, just talking to me. That would strengthen me so much. I thank God for Isaac being the young man of God that he is and what he's going to become for the glory of God in the last days. May God bless him all the days of his life and make Isaac always stay close to his grandmother that he loves. I love you very much Isaac and Luke and Jayden. God bless you all.

ISAAC ALLEN'S STORY

Hearing my grandparents had gotten the new virus COVID-19 started an interesting moment of my life at the age of sixteen years. I knew Massachusetts had been hit very hard with COVID-19; therefore, I feared the worst. Living in West Virginia, I had no say-so in what Grandmother would do. During the beginning stages of COVID-19 in the United States, I asked my grandmother to stay home, wash their hands, and be cautious in public areas.

However my grandmother Sara is a very strong, independent woman of God and does not listen too much to us. She will always continue her life as though nothing was wrong. As the number of cases grew, so did my anxieties and worries and fears. I felt like something was going to happen to her, and I was so worried. I didn't want her to be sick.

When my grandmother had advised me she was not feeling well, instantly my mind soared to the worst. I was very upset. Then one morning, they were taken to the hospital quickly. Grandpa was at the point of death when he could no longer breathe. All we could do was pray. Before my grandparents went to the hospital, I question my grandmother Sara.

"Grandma, will you please tell me—the truth can you smell anything? Please tell me. A prime sign of the virus is the loss of taste and smell." I waited for an answer as I drifted asleep. As soon as my eyes opened that morning, I woke up with the worst possible answer I did not want to read. The answer texted back to me was *no*.

I instantly knew at that second they had the coronavirus. I called her and checked on her every day during that time. Getting into FaceTime with her was very easy for me, knowing she was in good hands. I wished every day that my voice was there to cover her and my hugs to warm her. Even though we were 685 miles apart, I never felt closer to my grandparents. I'm looking forward to being with my grandparents another day shortly.

I am so proud of Isaac that he turned his fears back into joy and happiness that God brought us out of this. Can you imagine when he goes back to his high school, and he can tell his teachers about his grandparents and how went through this horrible disease—and how we lived?

CHAPTER 13

The Power of Prayer

You know the Bible says to pray without ceasing. It's important that you have a "PowerPoint" of prayer in your life every single day that you take very seriously.

We all have to give God time in prayer, for we are sinners who come short of the glory of God. He wants to hear our voices, giving Him praise, and we must honor Him and respect Him too. If you have prayerlessness in your life, you don't care about praying, you don't care about seeking the Lord, and you don't care about walking with Him, then how can He move for you, how can He set you free, and how can He be there for you?

It's so important that you have a relationship with Christ so that He will get you through any diseases, any pandemic, any COVID-19, and any sickness faster. His Word says He will make a way of escape, and you have to believe this.

If you are prayerless, and you don't believe in God, then you need to consider that maybe you need to try Jesus Christ.

Christians, you should always pray to God; if you do not pray, then it's called prayerlessness, which is a sin. We must seek His face; we must have the communion and fellowship with Him every single day. That is our strength, our joy, our happiness, and our healing. The power of prayer and fasting moves mountains. The Bible says if you pray and fast, you can say to any mountain: be removed and it shall be removed (Matthew 17:21). Fasting is the master key to the kingdom of God and protecting your family.

CHAPTER 14

Our Lord Let Us Live

The minute the nurse looked at me, she said to open up your window and smell that fresh air. That sounded strange to me because I just heard on the news that you must wear a mask and be careful breathing in the air because a virus may be in it. Then I'm heard a nurse say to open up the fresh air and breathe it; it's so wonderful for your lungs.

So I had her open up the window for me, and a gush of fresh air came in. I did not realize that's exactly what I needed. I needed to get all the toxins out of my lungs. I needed to breathe nothing but the good old fresh air that's in America. I was wondering if they made a mistake by telling us not to breathe the fresh air and wear a mask. I can understand if you're around a crowd of people that you need to be careful now because of the COVID-19.

But when you're all by yourself, sitting in the sun, you are okay. Then, all the sudden, they're telling you to put a mask on when you're walking by yourself with no one around, maybe on your own property with eighty acres of land, something's wrong with the air. I was really questioning this idea of opening up the window and let the wave of fresh air come in that window.

I never shut it. I left it open all night long. The room got really cold, but I just got under the blankets. I was not about to shut that window, and I was breathing so well. The next day, a different nurse came into the room when it was so cold. That nurse said we need to keep the windows shut. I thought, *Well, one said up and one said down. One was full of positive faith and one was full of fear*.

Then I realized the air in the room was not polluted. God gave us this air to breathe. When the rain come and the wind came, I do believe that God was purifying the land with the freshness of His glory. Our Lord let us live. And every day, whether it's raining, cold, snowing, or the sun is shining, fall, winter, or summer, I'm going to enjoy this fresh air.

When you go through the coronavirus and your when your air is blocked and you cannot hardly breathe, then whose report should you believe? It'd be different if a bomb went off, and you had to find shelter for protection. But that's not what happened. It was only a virus, a disease. There are many sickness and diseases in the world. I'll still would like to have an explanation why they felt like we had to cover our windows and not go outside in the air.

They're still saying it, and I'm watching children ride their bikes, and families are playing in the yard. Teenagers are sunbathing in their own yards. They do not look too sick; they look like they're getting fresh sun and fresh air. Go outside or take a walk, and enjoy the fresh air; everything is made by God. Take a deep breath and let this fresh air and sun heal your body.

When I go outside, I take a deep breath and start praising God, saying thank you. I see the leaves blowing, the sun shining, and the birds flying. when the birds are flying and they're not dropping to the ground, that lets me know they're not dying and that means there's fresh air. I do not see the animals dropping dead everywhere; I see them breathing fresh air.

I see them having fun in our world call the United States of America. And we need to enjoy the freedom of our fresh air. I never let anyone take it from us. Our Lord let us survive the COVID-19. I am a survivor. and I tell you the truth: the fresh air, the wind, and the sun are great for your lungs.

"For God didn't give us a spirit of fear but of power and love and a sound mind" 2 Timothy 1:7. And he gave us fresh air to breathe.

I'm watching the flowers coming out everywhere; the grass are turning greener, and the trees are blooming with new leaves on them. That shows me the fresh air is still real today. I see the flowers growing. They're living inside our world with fresh air, I don't see the flowers wilting and dying. I see the bees flying. Why does man put so much fear upon us in America?

When the coronavirus started, we went into a four-hour prayer at our church, with only four of us laying on the floor of the church, praying and seeking God. I heard the Lord say, "Look," and it would look like it was raining all over the world. I heard the Lord say, "Look closer." When I did that, raindrops burst open to the most beautiful flower, and the flower is called the Rose of Sharon. The Bible said He is the Rose of Sharon and the Lily of the Valley, and the bride is the Morning Star. God was showing me this at the springtime of the year.

On Easter Sunday, the resurrection, morning came and He had power over death, hell, and the grave—and even air when Jesus raised Lazarus from the dead.

Jesus also cleansed our world at the time of his celebration of what he did two thousand years ago, and it's called Resurrection Sunday. He started letting it rain all over, and I knew that God likes cleaning the world with his love because he loves us so much.

Man is trying to keep us in captivity, keep us in fear that if we walk outside, we're going to die. Well, that's a lie.

Our Lord brought from death to life. He breathed the breath of life in us to live again. And He has breathed the breath of life back into America. We must not take it for granted, and we must praise His glorious and wonderful name.

Go on outside and enjoy the fresh air because God made it, and He knows you're here, and He loves you.

CHAPTER 15

Be Very Well and Alert

It's very important that you take time and be really concerned about these hospitals, nursing homes, and facilities where your family members are staying. Today a TV station interviewed me in Massachusetts, and they were asking me about people scared of going into the nursing home in the hospitals.

I'm really concerned, and I want you to be alert aware of what's going on around your families. You need to take time and find someone that you know or get a close friend who may know someone that's in the medical field to help you with any situation that may arise that you don't quite understand when the doctors do not give you clear understanding. You can also go to your person that you have selected on the outside to look up medical terms and find out what's going on. Do not take for granted that what the doctors or nurses are saying about what is on paper. They may all say they're doing good, but deep down they may not be doing good, and you need to know all information, such as their vitals. You need to know everything about your loved one's care.

How much are families are taken care of, even in the nursing homes. Wherever your loved one is, just make sure you're alert about everything. Remember the doctors and the nurses are doing their jobs. I give God the glory for them, I think they do a wonderful job, but there are some that are there just for a paycheck. They don't have the heart for life or for the patient like they need to.

I had not been in the hospital for thirty-seven years or more all because I had so much faith in God, and that was the time I needed to give birth to my son. Because God has been so good to me over these years, I must have been so focused on the building the kingdom of God that I did not realize what was happening in the government.

I do know that God had me in the spin cycle years ago, and I felt like I was drying out because the Bible says God is the Potter, and I am the clay.

Sometimes we get reshaped for His glory and then we don't realize what's going on in the government of the world. I hope you understand what I'm trying to say, and then you see things for what they really are. The Lord allowed me to see what was going on in the world system, but it's been thirty-eight years since I'd been in the hospital.

Thirty-eight years ago, hospital staff really truly loved their patients; they were expected to unconditionally love, and things were just different. Sure, I saw that when I was in the hospital while having my children, but what I saw was in the hospital this time took me into reality. The Lord showed me what was going on with employees; maybe that's why the Lord took me in the hospital.

Some things are just not right, and you had better watch your family and be alert. Don't be asleep or passive of what's going on when your family goes in any institution or any situation, actually, any place. Be alarmed and be alert and be very sensitive, cautious, and very clear; understand what's going on with your loved ones.

While I stress this, I know we have some great workers in the hospitals and doctors and nurses. They save lives every day, and we give God glory for them. We definitely pray for them every single day that they'll be strengthened and used by God to help protect the people.

But then you have people in there, who are evil, and they need to repent and be saved. I was shocked that they were scared of the coronavirus I had and used verbal words to bring me down in an uncaring way. Not all of them were like that, just a few, but they are the ones you have to watch for.

When I first arrived at the hospital, the woman who was working on me was so busy. I do not know her name or anything about her, but I knew she was very sweet and very kind. I could see that she had a lot of love for patients, and I could tell that she really knew her job. And I was so glad that she was there, working on me. But I was shocked at the doctor who opened up the door but never came in to examine me. He just told me what they plan to do for me.

I watched the precious nurse who did all the work. The doctor really never said hello or asked me how I was. I can remember he just opened up the door and he said they would send me home, saying "My team thinks you have the coronavirus, the test they had did that day would come back in four days. They did confirm I had double pneumonia.

The doctor was going to send me home, but Cindy and Paige, our "family" members, said absolutely not. I was so sick. The doctor told me to do what I want to do, and then he shut the door. Lord, help me. It was Paige who spoke up and said, "I'd never seen Pastor so sick in my life. You need to keep her and observe her well for one night."

I don't think the doctor remembered that I had just come into the emergency room by an ambulance and laying on the stretcher.

My husband's going to give his testimony at the end of the of the book. It is amazing how he survived COVID-19.

If I had not had someone that was alert and aware of the medical terms, I would have not known what would had happen to Donnie. I probably would have just agreed with the doctor. I would have noted the spirit but not anything about the medical field. So we had to be aware of everything that was going on. And that's what got us through the COVID-19.

If the doctors and nurses say this is what we're going to do and , then you can talk to them in a very kind of voice, but you ask them to explain this in plan un medical words—what's going on so you can understand. If you can have someone who is med-ical there, who knows the terms, they can shake their head no and say that's not right. We need something better. Then usually they do what's best for the family.

So take time and be alert and be aware and be very cautious and find out what's going on with your family and yourself get the medical records. Do everything to see that your family and your self is being taken very good care of the right way.

If they are in the nursing home, are they been treated right? Have they been well fed? Do they have security cameras that you can look at to see if they're okay? Are they any bruises on your family member?

With my husband, I kept asking whether they were giving him chest PT and whether they were giving him breathing treatments. They would always say yes, we're doing this, but then we found out they were not. That a shame they wanted me to listen what they wanted me to hear and accept it. But if you have someone who is there and they know you know medical terms, then they will get on the same page with you, and everything will get done quickly. Then your family will get out of the hospital much faster. You're not being smart and you're not being hateful; you're just trying to save your own family's life. I do believe a lot of people with COVID-19 may not have died if they would had t someone on the outside to help them and fight for them.

Even when you get your family member home, you need to make sure that someone knows what they're saying to you over the phone, Or video chat And you know that they are doing exactly what's best for your loved one. When my husband got home, I had to tell the doctor that I wanted him to get another chest x-ray. That was almost two weeks after he returned home. The doctor said it was going to take a month for him to get one. I pressed in and said he was the worst case in the hospital, and he needs a another chest x-ray and he cannot wait one more month. The doctor said she just didn't think it would be possible, but I said she was going to have to make it possible.

Well I had the x-rays done that day because she heard my voice. This is what I wanted done that day for my husband with him standing there. Sometimes we have to tell them what's best for our loved ones because the medical people do not live in our homes, and they do not see what we see. The same thing with the medication. Also if you don't feel like it's right you must say this doesn't feel right; I want it done right. This is your family and you need to see to through. This was my love of forty-eight years. I was not about to let anything go wrong. I wanted it done right.

And when they hear your voice then they say they've got someone helping them; they're not alone.

If you can have someone in the medical field right at your kitchen table, helping you get these things done, then use them to help you make sure everything is correct. Again, I stress this is your loved one, your whole world.

You only have one family in life take very good care of them and God will always bless you.

CHAPTER 16

ICE

As a short summary in this chapter, I just want to talk about a cup of ice or a glass of ice.

We heard on the news that you were not supposed to have anything with ice in it when you had COVID-19. I went up to one of the stores to buy a bag of ice, and they said they were not allowed to sell ice.

While I was going through the sickness, I wanted ice, though I was told I was not supposed to have ice but only hot drinks. I had drunk so much hot stuff I did not want no more. I wanted something ice cold. I went to go get a bag of ice, but they said I could not get it because it was pulled from the cooler, so we they cannot sell it. I thought that's crazy. But I started drinking hot drinks.

I felt my throat getting more swollen and thick and making me cough more. I said, "I keep coughing more because this stuff is so hot. This does not feel right." I started freezing my water bottles, and then I started drinking it cold and I noticed the swelling started going down in my throat. When I arrived at the hospital, the first thing they gave me was ice chips. I noticed that while I was in the hospital had one cup of hot tea and it started making me cough real bad and it started making my throat swell. So what in the world was up with that? I would like to know the truth on this. All I took in the hospital was ice cold, but even after I got home. When I got home, I was drinking nothing but ice-cold drinks—as cold as I could stand them. I want to say the idea of hot drinks was diagnosed completely wrong, and it made the people more sick because it was too hot. I had the reversed the swelling when I had the cold drinks.

Personal Testimony of Both Pastors: Donnie Is Alive

I t's truly a miracle that my husband came home alive. Donnie began to talk to me, by saying, "I would not wish this COVID-19 on my own enemy. This covid-19 is so evil. I'm so glad to be home, Sara, and I'm so glad that I'm out of the hospital. I just don't want to be a really big burden on you after you have been also sick because you have got a lot to take care of now, with me still having to fight to live.

"I'm so glad that you picked me up from the hospital that day. When I saw your face, I knew that I was going to live. As the nurse wheeled me down the hallway in the wheelchair, I was still gasping for every breath with my oxygen tank that I had to fight for that morning. They were releasing me with no oxygen to go home. I was wondering why in the world I would go home without any oxygen tanks. Then I said that I was having a difficult time breathing, and my oxygen was dropping down to 84 to 87, but I would have to fight real hard to get it back up to the 90s. I have been so sick with this COVID-19 plus pneumonia; you could never imagine how very serious this demon would desperately try to take over my lungs. And the demon plans were to try to kill me. But I fought so hard I kept speaking: my Anchor holds.

As I barely got into the van, I could see the doctors were ready to let me go. I was so glad that I was going home. I told God it was up Him now. When I got into the van, I did not have shoes on. I had just the slippers that they gave me in the hospital.

I struggled hard to get in my van seat, seeing my beautiful wife standing there grinning with everything she had and saying, "My baby, I am taking you home, and everything's going to be okay." Hearing her courageously say at that moment, "We are the survivors of the COVID-19 and the devil did not kill us. The Lord let us live," encouraged me.

But she did not know what type of mess I was still in mentally and physically, though my spirit was strong. I can see her eyes looking at me just smiling and laughing. She was so happy that I was coming home. She welcomed me home with such love, saying we're having a Jubilee party every day for weeks, praising God We were having a Jubilee party because Jesus Christ let us live.

She would cook a little dinner and make it into a joyful Jubilee party. Sara would prepare my meals three times a day plus all of my snacks, and even through the challenge she had to go through, she always did it with a smile. But, I can see in her eyes she was getting tired too, and I could hear her praying and sometimes crying to God. What she had to go through to get me back on my feet was amazing, and this is my testimony.

What I am telling you is the truth. It is how my God gave my wife strength and gave me strength and patience to endure.

I was so glad to be getting out of the hospital. I felt like the doctor wanted me out of the hospital. However, before I left the hospital, the precious nurses came running into my room one Tuesday morning. They said, "Donnie your oxygen has dropped down to 70. What's going on?" And they kept working with me and working with me and they kept saying, "Boy, you are in a mess. We know they released you from intensive care, but we do not understand why your oxygen keeps dropping. Are you okay? Do you understand why?" I told them I didn't know why.

They would get it back up to the 80s, and then they would turn the oxygen tank back up to 10. I said do not know why my oxygen keeps dropping. A very sweet nurse kept coming in and rubbing my shoulders, saying, "It's going to be okay; just breathe." Then she would proceed to say, "Sir, you are in a mess. But we are here to help you." At that time I did not know if they were thinking that I was going to die again or what. I felt like I was because I could not breathe.

Then my oxygen suddenly would go back up and then I had a wonderful day. And then on that Friday I was going to be released from the hospital, and the respiratory therapist came in, and she said, "Donnie, you do not need to take any oxygen home. It is good."

I said, "Ma'am, I cannot breathe."

They she said I looked good, and I felt good, but then all the sudden, when I sat up or stood up, my oxygen dropped to the bottom. I would reply to her again to the respiratory therapist, "I cannot go home without any oxygen; I cannot breath. I have to have it to breathe!"

She finally saw that I was really telling her the truth and struggling. She said, "Well, I will send it home with you," and she put the order in.

Thank God, she did. Today I'm still on oxygen, and it's has been over a month since I came home. God had healed me of the coronavirus and helped me with so much more.

God has been so good to me. Now I'm walking up fourteen steps by myself without my wife and Paige who had to hold me, almost carrying me, up the steps for weeks after I arrived home. Praise the Lord because my anchor holds.

I want to go back to when I was in the hospital now and tell you what happened. Again, I do not wish the COVID-19 on my own enemy. I never want to go through this again.

While I was in the hospital, I was so sick, my mind went every direction. All the medication may have also contributed to that. I kept dreaming stupid, crazy stuff. I was so very sick, and all I was trying to do was just breathe and live—at every breath.

I had to sleep on one side or my stomach so I could at least breathe. I was dreaming; then I was delusional. I felt like I was in a master storm. The storm seemed so real that I was actually seeing this happen before my eyes. My body was even straight out from the storm, holding on to what looked like a pole, but I was out like a robe, but it was like a master anchor I was holding on to. And I kept saying, "My anchor holds, Lord." Even though the storm was pulling me this way and that way and from side to side, slamming me from left to right, with a 200-mile-an-hour wind when I was trying to catch my breath. Every second and every minute, the water was overflowing me.

The wind was so hard and pulled me from the anchor so that I did not think I was going to be able to hold on so many times. I could feel myself coming apart inside and out. This one was so strong that it was actually trying to pull me away from the anchor, and I was holding with every strength I could. I was determined not to let go. And I knew that the anchor was Jesus Christ; I was holding on to Him.

And I was crying out to God, "Please help me. Please, God, help me." As the storms keep raging and raging and raging, I almost let go several times. But I kept holding on just barely with what strength of faith I had.

I kept crying out to God, You are faithful; You're not going to leave me in this condition because my anchor holds. Lord, I thank you for the healing power. I am thank you for helping me, and I'm trusting You will not leave me here in this hospital. But you are going to let me go home and be with my wife again and my family, aren't you, Lord?"

I was waiting on Him, I never blamed Him, and I never was upset with Him, with all He was doing. I was still having my faith in God. I knew that God was faithful.

I would like to thank God for the nurses and the doctors who did help me. But I did have a doctor who treated me, that when he walked in my room, I could feel the evil that was around him. I could tell that he did not want to help me. I'm beginning to find out after I arrived home from Paige and my wife Sara that that particular doctor would not prescribe the proper medicine. And my wife started fighting for me to get me on the Hydroxycholorquine. She found out that they were not giving it to me and other medications that I really needed. Even a nurse had spoken to her and said they did not understand why the doctor was doing this to me they told her I was the worst case there, and the doctor refused to put me on this medication and the Z-pack, which I seriously needed.

So my wife and Paige kept asking questions over the phone to know my status. My status grew worse. My wife and Paige really got the hospital's attention. Did they knew I was dying?

Sara said, "Enough is enough! I want my husband on this *now*! She was pleading with the hospital to help me. Can you imagine I'm lying in the bed, and I did not even know anything that was going on because I was just too sick to know.

I was too sick to breathe, I was too sick to eat, and I was too sick to get up out of bed or even think about anything. I was in a master storm. And then my wife proceeded to tell me when I got home from the hospital all she had to do and how she was also fighting for me on the phone after I got out of the hospital. Remember I was not allowed to have any visitors, not even my wife, to come in during lockdown. I know when I was admitted into the hospital from the emergency room, they told me I had double pneumonia. I did not know at the time that I had the coronavirus because my test results would not come back for three days. But they assumed that I did, and I figured I did. They started me on the antibiotics in the beginning, but then they stopped real quick, per this doctor.

Plus in my own body I went into more challenges. I went into liver failure and heart congestive failure Plus, I had the hospital pneumonia as well as a blood clot in my lung. My wife Sara and our daughters had to express strongly to get me on the right medication to make sure I came out of this storm. Definitely we had to live, knowing that God was bringing us out of this storm.

My wife and Paige also expressed that she would like me to have antibiotics and also have chest PTs and extra to have the best care. Sara and Paige wanted the doctor to listen them to get me better quickly.

She knew she could not come and visit me, and it was really hard for her. She wanted to visit me and pray with me and anoint me with anointing with oil and have communion with me and to hold me and love and tell me everything was going to be all right.

Even though she's a register chaplain, she was not even allowed to come in. She was even the chaplain in the hospitals in West Virginia.

I could hear my wife telling me these things on the phone the best way she could, knowing the condition that I was in. I was too sick to speak with her, and also I could not get my breath to talk to her. But I really enjoyed hearing her voice, telling me that she loved me. She would always tell me, "Honey, the Lord is bringing you home." She believed it. And I kept telling her, "Please do not leave me in here; whatever you do, please do not leave me in here."

I knew that was going to be a big challenge for her, but she is always up for a big challenge. She will face anything and engage in the fight to win the victory to be able to say that God was able to take care of the situation. And He was faithful. I've seen God use her as a general to fight. She fights to the very end until she wins the battle to victory.

To my surprise I did not know anything that was going on inside the hospital. Sara kept it from me so I would not worry. I could not express any concerns to my wife. Sara was always telling me not to talk and just listen. She would remind me that I was breathing too hard and that I was not able to talk to her. But she wanted me to listen to her voice. She would express to me how much she loved me and that everything was going to be okay. She would sing to me at times.

Then during one phone call, she began to explain they were having to repeatedly ask the doctor to give me certain medications, but I never said anything back because I was too sick to talk. To my surprise, they told me I was going to get to see my wife on an iPad; your wife wants to see me. So the doctor and the head nurse came into my room. They both stood on opposite sides of the bed, and to my surprise, they helped me up out of the bed and said I needed to tell my wife and daughter to back off.

And they began to say to me, "Do you know what's going on? Are you telling your wife stuff to get them to talk to us and then telling us something different?" At that moment I did not know anything that was being said or what going on. All I knew is that I was trying to breathe every second and to live. I did not know anything that was happening. When they asked me to please tell my wife back off, I became very scared! I do not get scared a lot, and I did not have fear at that moment. However, I knew that doctor hated me, I felt that doctor hated me from the first time he came into my room. But then I realized right then he really did not want to take care of me, and what I was feeling was correct.

I could barely breath or even move in my bed. I had five different medical things happening to me, I'm in a terrible storm, and this doctor and the head nurse are asking me all kinds of questions and telling me to tell my wife of forty-eight years who knows me more than anybody, as well as Paige, to back off.

When I saw my wife for the first time in many days and she was looking at me on the iPad, I can see her smile. She kept telling me she loved me. Everything was going to be all right and she was bringing me home soon. But then, she proceeded to tell me after I got home from the hospital that she could tell I was scared to death when the doctor and nurse were beside you. She told me I could tell her now.

Sara said to me, "Your eyes were going back and forth back and forth, and I knew you were trying to tell me something. You had a frozen fright look on your face, having been given orders you couldn't understand." That was the first time we'd seen each other in two weeks. And then all the sudden I'd been given orders by the nurse and the doctor, and I did not know what was going on. I did not understand what was going on, and I was as sick as a dog in the bed.

I knew that I was about to die, and they were more concerned about something my wife said than about my care at that time. Dear Lord! After that evening, I never saw that doctor or that nurse again. I'd received a new doctor and a new nurse who came in to my room and cared for me. She said, "You have been here for a couple weeks. I want to let you shower today you have not had one since you have been here. We will have a nurse be help you to shower." She was so nice to me. I felt peace then, and she was very caring. I could see this nurse cared, and she was trying to help me from that moment on.

The warm shower felt so wonderful that day. Then they helped me back in the bed. I decided to order some food, and then I realized I was feeling a little bit better. I walked around my bed. I felt stronger and was thinking, *Wow, maybe I can be home soon!*

A few hours later, something happened.

VISION OF THE COVID-19 DEMON

I was sitting on the side of my bed and was thanking God for bringing me out of this storm, and then all sudden, something changed. I looked and I saw the Coronavirus demon look at me. He was real small and the color of brand-new motor oil that you would put in the car. He was shaped like the letter Z, and his eyes were shaped like a snake's. This spirit spoke out to me and said, "I am not finished with you yet."

At that moment my life went into a whirlwind, and I felt sicker than I ever had. By that evening, I was in the bed again, and my life was going into a downward spin to death. By the next morning, I was rushed into it the intensive care unit. I did not know if I was going to live or die. At that moment, I just knew that I was so cold and so very sick. And I was shaking all over, gasping for my breath every second. I really felt death all around me at that moment. I did not care if I really lived or died. But I knew I needed help quickly, and that help had to come from only God. He was my only hope and my chance to live.

In intensive care, my oxygen dropped down below 70. The nurse came running in with some other nurse to help me. She came in my room quickly and brought a lot of warm covers and kept putting them on top of me to keep my body warm, but my body was freezing. I was dying at that moment. I could hardly breathe, and then an older nurse came and upped my oxygen to 10. She looked at me with her sad eyes, and she said, "Honey, you are in a horrible mess. Do not do anything; just try to stay as still as you can in this bed."

In my mind I figured she was thinking this man's not going to be here long. All I could see was the raging storm that was blowing all around me And I was still holding on to the anchor as tight as I could. I could not really take this fighting to breathe anymore. I knew there was nothing to breathe in my lungs, and I knew there was no room for air. I was so packed up with double pneumonia and the coronavirus sickness, and I was actually fighting to breathe night after night ever since I had come into that hospital.

This sickness, coronavirus, had taken over my lungs quickly to kill me. It attacked me and took over my breathing. The demon was laughing that he could.

I was thinking within myself, *I was all alone.*

I starting to talk to myself: "Donnie you are in a real bad shape. Only the hand of God will pull me out of this." I was in the storm, and I knew that Jesus Christ was my strong Anchor.

There was really no air going into my lungs at all, just to my throat. It was really in my mouth and just out. The doctor saw this, and he said, we need to go and put you on the ventilator machine, Mr. Price."

I said, "Just wait a little bit. I'm breathing okay."

I started faking my breathing. I did not want him to put me on this machine. Then the nurse said, "I do not think he needs this right now. Let's wait a little bit and give him some time," and the doctor listened to him.

The doctor said, "He is not doing well and won't last long. Then he said to me, "Mr. Price, I'm going to give you a few more hours, and then we'll will see how you are doing. Right now, you have no air going into your lungs."

I kept telling him, "Oh yes I do." I kept faking my breathing in front of him to make him think I was really getting air in my lungs, but I really was not. So I was trying everything possible in my own power not to let them put me on a ventilator. I did not want to go on this machine, but I was at the point that I knew I was going to have to do something, and I was going to have to let them do it soon.

I had to keep pushing fear back all the time, and then I had to speak and think constantly in faith, even when I was in the bed. I had to walk by faith and believe *without fear* when just oxygen was brought in my nose, and there just only air going to my nose, and everything else is closed up.

When I arrived into the intensive care, there stood the breathing machine in my room. They were ready to put me on the ventilator right then. But God had a plan. The Holy Ghost spoke to me and told me not to let them put me on that machine, and I was trying every way possible to do obey Him. I had enough awareness of what was going on and what they were going to do to me. The Holy Ghost said, *"You will* lose all control if you let them have the control *over your life*; then Satan would have *control over you."*

I was ready to go on it because I could not take it no longer. I remember a wonderful male nurse who had faith, and I do believe the Lord sent him here from North Carolina to help me. Remember what the Bible says: life and death in power of your own tongue. Truly by the hand of God, I'm still living today, and I give him all the praise and all the glory.

While I was in the storm, I started drifting so strongly, and it was a matter of life and death. Then all of a sudden, a very sweet voice came to me and the peace of God was amazing. It filled the whole room. Right then I saw the hand of the Lord reach out to me, and He spoke to me, "If you want to, you can let go and rest now, Donnie. You can come and be with Me; it will be all right. If you want to go with Me, just let go now! He was giving me permission to let go and take his hand and go with Him because He was the anchor standing in front of me. I know it was Jesus Christ giving me permission to let go and come to be with Him and He would take me to heaven where I will spend eternity.

I saw my life, and I was ready to go. I was ready to die, but then I realized there was something I needed to do. There was some work I had to get done; it was so important. I needed to stay here and help Sara, my wife.

I asked Him, "Is it okay if I stay here and help Sara?"

And then suddenly, the storm stopped; everything ceased, and I woke up and realized that my breathing had improved. I knew that the Lord had touched me, and He had healed me of the coronavirus. He had removed that demon away from me and set me free (Ps. 91:10).

They released me from intensive care on Sunday. I was in own room by Monday, and on Tuesday, another storm tried to hit me again—my oxygen dropped suddenly. We knew that God had brought us this far and that God had a plan, so we kept our eyes focused on what the Lord was going to do next.

Sara will talk now!

My husband has made a tremendously healing progress because of the kingdom of God.

While he was in the hospital

That's why it's important that you have lions around you. Then, if you do get in circumstances and you need to know the status of your family member's life, they will be right there with you and know everything that's going on.

I'm so thankful for Paige and my family also for the support they have given me.

Before my husband left the hospital they had tested him twice to make sure he did not have the coronavirus, and his tests came back negative. They released him from the hospital, and he was getting into the van. I was so excited I could not hardly stand it. I ran out to the van and was trying to help him get into the vehicle. He had his little oxygen tank trying to get into the van, and then I realized that he's not breathing that well. "Lord, help him, and, God, you are going to make a way where there seems to be no way."

No one, not the hospital or the doctors or anyone ever told me how bad he was, emerging from the emergency room that day. They never take the covid-19 patients out of the emergency room exit for some reason, but that day they did. We don't know why. They said he was just ready to come home. I was not equipped or prepared or had even experienced anything like this. I had to educate myself really fast about oxygen tanks and medication and proper care for him within one day or more—to understand what in the world was going on. It took a lot of self-training within the next few days to understand how in the world to help him to get him to breathe properly.

I could feel the Holy Spirit within me, leading me and telling me what I needed to do. I had to be very calm and ready for anything that that might arrive suddenly. I had just come out the hospital myself.

Paige was the most wonderful support person to have around to encourage and direct me and show me what to do. She also had a positive attitude and a lot of laughter, a lot of joy, while helping me on what I needed to do. She made sure he had the proper care. And to make sure that he would stay alive she would also work consistently with him.

Many times it would scare her half to death and thought we were going to losing him, but then all the sudden he would just bounce right back. And then we started praising God and taking own deep breaths back in our own lives, saying, "Dear God, help us. And also, we thank Jesus."

You just couldn't return to the hospital if you wanted to go back to the emergency room just to get a recheck, that was impossible. That just did not happen during the pandemic. You are on your own!

We learned that everything will level out suddenly! And we knew he was going to live that day. We were not about to put him back in the hospital. We were making plans to take him to a larger hospital if we had to, so he could really get some help.

But as we showed him love every day, giving it to him it liberally, it brought that loving and healing to him much faster. And he would call us his two angels.

We had a wonderful social worker who called, and I always explained to her about our my situation. She was shocked also that the hospital did this to us.

She even saw his records and was looking at the X-ray of his lungs and could not believe that he was home. She got us nurses and a respiratory therapist who started coming to the house immediately. She wanted to make sure that we had the proper medication too.

I finally got his primary doctor on the phone for him to do a video chat to be able to help him and to get through this process. She was also very surprised that he came home. She looked at him and said, "You bit the bullet. How in the world did you do this since you're the first patient that I know that came out of the hospital. Everyone else in your condition passed away. She proceeded to tell us what we needed to do that he would have to go through in the next few weeks that helped him some.

And boy, was I not ready, but God helped me through this to get him to the place that he was completed healed. Donnie was healed of the coronavirus, as his test showed. He was healed of double pneumonia. He also had a small blood clot in his lung that came because of the coronavirus. And the nurse told me in our home that he got the strain of hospital pneumonia on top of everything as well, and that was the worst case of pneumonia, as she said.

I had respiratory therapist come in and help him also. They did come, maybe twice a week. And they was very helpful and very kind and very sweet. Paige and I would work with him consistently. I mean literally twenty-four-hour care I had to push everything out of the way that was surrounding me, even the church and everything else to make sure that I could stay focused just on his well-being and his health and also his life.

They said they we're going to send him to a rehabilitation center, but the hospital said that the rehabilitation center will not take him. I have no clue why. But I remember what the Lord told my son, that his dad would be coming home on the following week. And the Lord blocked everything that could be blocked and brought him home. So we could take care of him and get him back on his feet.

I do know through that process I learned to understand families that have loved ones that are home and in need of twenty-four-hour care. I was thankful for the Lord to learn this.

I did not know when he was released from the hospital how serious his life was shattered into pieces and how God would give us strength to put our lives back together again so quickly with his guidance.

CHAPTER 18

Hearing Him Gasping for Breath

When my husband arrived home, we noticed quickly that something was totally different and very wrong about him. Paige and I would start talking to him, and he was totally different. And then she said, "Oh my God, he's got PTSD (post-traumatic stress disorder)."

We felt like it was from the doctor who pulled him up out of the bed and scared him. We do not know what happened, but we do know when he arrived home, he was not the same man, so we had to work on this PTSD as well as the other areas in his life that needed to be healed. I was ready for this challenge. I had my baby home. And that's all that mattered in this world.

When he first arrived from home, he was healed from the COVID-19 that was proven in the hospital. The hospital had him tested two times more.

He did had double pneumonia in the worst way. Anybody could have pneumonia, but he also had hospital pneumonia, and he also had a blood clot and now added PTSD. He also had a cholesterol level that was so low that it was in the danger point. He had liver failure, plus he had heart failure in the hospital.

My husband had lost over 20 pounds through the sickness. He had not had a shaved and bathed only one time. And he look like a grizzly bear. He had a frightened look in his eyes.

I decided that just as quick as I can get him up and help him. The first thing we needed to do was to get him a bath and a shave. That was some doing with an oxygen tank running.

At first, I just washed him myself and just nursed him quietly so he could get a adjusted to being home. The shock of everything is amazing. No one expects the shock the impact of the

COVID-19. How do we teach him how to eat again? And was it okay to eat? After a few days, I finally got him to go into the shower one morning. I said, "Come on, we're going to do this together." And I went in there with him and bathed him from top to bottom and helped him.

And then I was able to cut that long beard off and get him cleaned up, and boy, did he say that felt so good, and he was happy to have hot shower. This went on for about a week, and then all the sudden, one morning I saw him, and he was able to bath himself, and he did a very good job.

When your family members are sick always give them much praise. Never put them down but praise them. And I was praising him always through the progress that he was doing. And we constantly told him how proud we were of him.

When any distractions come around, you just cannot listen to it. Just listen to what is going on in your own house, and take care of that situation. That is all that really matters. Everything else will fall into place in due time, especially if you are a pastor. I saw his frail little face looking at me and trying to smile. That said a lot to me.

Remember I just got out of the hospital myself and trying also to take care of myself, plus making sure that he was taken care of. I asked God to give me strength.

One morning I was running out of the bathroom from the shower, and discovered he could not breathe. I worked on him until he finally got stable and was able to breath well that morning. And then in the next three hours, I was supposed to be in the pulpit, preaching the Gospel to the congregation by live streaming, knowing this was my second time back to work.

I could hear him breathing, "Sara, help me." As I was running toward him, my eyes started tearing up. it was 7 o'clock in the morning. I started doing chest PTs on his back, turning his oxygen up, trying to get his oxygen perfusion back up, keeping him breathing, giving him a breathing treatment. Then all the sudden, I burst out saying, "I am praising God for helping us. I am thanking you, God. Please help him." And then he just coughed up a big mess of stuff.

Then he said to me, "I can breathe now!" And I was crying and thanking the Lord for helping us. And then He was fine. It takes about forty minutes to an hour to work with him every morning.

Then I'm sitting at the kitchen table finally and catching my own breath after that bad episode that he just had in his own bed. I just dropped my head into my face and started crying. "Lord, how can I even preach today with what I just experienced? It took everything out of me." With a coronavirus, people don't understand that it takes a lot of rest after you get over it, and then you do get weak really quickly.

But everyone thinks that pastors or evangelists or apostles are supposed to always be strong. Well, we do have our moments also! We try not to show our weakness, but when we are weak, God makes us strong through Him. We have to be strong to make sure that our congregation is very strong and that they also are fed the Word of God to be able to make it through in their own lives and families. We are the pastors that preach and teach you how to have faith and miracles and how to be strong and how to know that God is still an on-time God.

We as pastors, evangelists, apostle, and teachers have to hear your concerns. We do hear so many people complain about this and that, and they do not realize what you have been through that morning. God, please forgive them. Then you put on a big smile, saying by faith we can do everything by His strength. We can do everything by His love. At the moment, when you are at setting at the table all by yourself with no one to talk to and no one around you, that's when you have to reach in for that faith for your own self.

I started praising God that morning for bringing him out of it again. Even though God delivered me of COVID-19 and the pneumonia, I have had to put myself aside and say, "Sara, you cannot think just of yourself. You have to think of him and the Lord and the people that you are about to face today. You are going on live streaming in just two hours. Your own congregation and strangers you do not even know are going to needing your attention."

And all I want to do is to be in a fetal position and cry to God, "Where are you at?" knowing he's been there all the time. I had to pull myself together quickly, shake off those heavy bands of sadness, quit crying, and hurry and get dressed. I fixed up my hair and got ready to get out the door. I had to remind myself of my own motto that we have in the church: "I cannot do anything, but I pitch out the barrels of the anointing of Jesus Christ, and He does all the work and He gets all the glory." That morning I was totally relying on the Lord Jesus Christ to help me and to bring His Word through me and to serve and help the people. And I can surely tell you this: he was an on-time God.

For God to use me or anyone else, we have to have a clean vessel in our lives and had the right mind and the right heart to say yes. I had to pull myself together that morning, and my plans changed. My plans that morning had changed suddenly. I had a different plan; my agenda was to slip out of the bed, get dressed a little bit early, and let him sleep. We were going to have a great morning. I could not wait to run to a quiet place downstairs that was on my mind and to spend time with the Lord. I wanted Him to know that I did not forget about Him as well. I am talking about time in prayer with the Lord.

I was trying so hard to get my prayer time in and to please Him also. My plans changed in an instant. I needed to help my husband, and it is real funny this did not happen the day before church, but it happened that day of church. All I wanted to do was to be still after that. I did not have enough strength to preach. I do not know if I could preach today.

But what I truly wanted was just to go back upstairs and curl beside my husband's arm and lay the whole day with him, just telling him how much I love him and everything's going to be okay.

That's where real faith comes in and says you have to believe in the impossible through the storm, through everything, because you can make it today. I felt a strong peace come over me, and I knew God was saying, "Everything's going to be all right. I've got you."

I want to say to my husband even through this process of this storm, "What we had to going through had been extremely bad and hard. Honey, this has made me a strong wife for you even more."

Through Jesus Christ, I could see the grace and the wisdom of God. I could see the love that I have for him. He was saying, "Everything's is going to be okay, Sara. I'm going to help you through this."

Whatever happened to Donnie in the hospital or out of the hospital, we may never know! But I do know this: my husband was not in this bad a condition when he left my house that day to go to the hospital.

Every day since he's come home, he's had an oxygen problem. And also we have had very special days as well. One day, I caught him in the garage, trying to be normal, trying to work with his oxygen tank beside him. He was trying to straighten up and clean the garage just like the real Donnie that I know. I could see Donnie wanted to go back to work so badly in his mind. And he was trying so hard, and he's pushing so hard. I have never seen a man push so hard to get off the oxygen like he has. And I know God has been faithful to help him.

His primary doctor and the nurses are so astounded. How fast he has come through this progress has been so unbelievable. Never give up on your loved ones; they need help, and we have to help them until they get back on their feet with God's strength.

I will never forget that day when the doctor looked at me and him and asked us, "How did you do this? You were the only one that I knew that left the hospital in this condition. You really bit the bullet," she said. "I'm looking at your records, Donnie. I'm looking at your X-ray. There is no way possible in this world that you should have walked out of that hospital; you should have been in the morgue. And you won the battle." We pointed up to the heavens and said, "God had this one, and He's the reason that we're both alive."

I received the CD containing my husband's x-rays of his lungs. It shows the amazing transformation, all due to the miracle of the healing power of the almighty God. And God gave him new Lungs. When God says yes to your healing, you are healed, and we give Him all the glory.

Every day I was happy to smile at him, and my smile was real in my heart. I knew God had already done his miracle, even though at times we had our ups and downs. I cried personal tears but had no fears. I laugh in joy every day when I wake up and see him lying there and know that he is alive. And I give God the glory when I lie in the bed and I turn to see my husband. Every day when he is sound asleep and I wake up, I thank God he's still with me.

Every day I remind my husband that God has this. No matter what you're going through, God has this for you and your family as well and your loved ones. Always take your special moment yourself and let it all out, and then go and enjoy your family. When you walk in the room and you see that big smile on your loved one's face like I did, that day is priceless, even though you have been through it. And then you hear him whistle and say, "Hey, good looking. You are still my baby doll." That's worth it all; that's worth everything that you have been through.

I remind the devil all the time he is a liar and the father of all lies. For our God has won this battle two thousand years ago to victory when Jesus was beaten and bruised for our healing. So many people receive their salvation but not their healing. Please receive your healing; it belongs to you today.

Because I trusted in the Lord and went into my own DNA of God, I'm alive because of him.

I still left my three Bibles at the doors of our home where God told me to leave them, open them, and do not move them. The Bibles are still there today.

There were three of us who got sick with the COVID-19 that was in my home, and all three are alive. I am a coronavirus survivor, and so is my husband, and we owe our lives to our Lord Jesus Christ.

John 3:16 says, "For God so loved the world that he gave his only son whosoever call upon the name of the Lord should not perish but have everlasting life." Jesus Christ is the only peace you are going to ever have.

It's very important for individuals to repent and accept Jesus as their Lord God and Savior because we do not know which day will be our last day upon this earth. We are praying for you, and we are praying for your families. May God Bless you.

Pastor Donnie Price, Survivor of the Coronavirus

CHAPTER 19

Paige's Personal Testimony

As a medical provider, I'm used to working around sick patients. I've worked in a hospital setting for over 6 years and my experience includes doing admissions in the ER and working in the Progressive care unit (PCU). My years of experience had left me battle-tested, but not jaded. I'd like to think of myself as a compassionate person who has always empathized with my patients. However, nothing could've adequately prepared me for what I was going to experience next.

In hindsight, when my pastors told me they weren't feeling well, I should of known something was very very wrong. They never complain. Never. So when Pastor Sara told me that she and Pastor Donnie weren't feeling that great earlier in the week, that should've sounded the alarm. I should've came over immediately. But I didn't. On Wednesday I checked in with my pastors and asked if I could come over and walk the dog to help them out. They accepted my request.

As soon as I walked into the door, I was in shock. I saw both of my pastors appearing ill. Pastor Donnie was sitting in a sofa in the living room. He was diaphoretic looking, pale, mildly short of breath and he was continuously coughing. Pastor Sara, though ill-appearing, didn't look as sick as Pastor Donnie. She was running back and forth trying to tend to her husband despite being ill herself.

I nervously did a few things in the kitchen, walked the dog and tried to help out with little things in the house. At that moment I understood why people say as a medical provider, you should never treat your own family. Sometimes it is so hard to tell them what to do. Other times you don't want to believe that they are as sick as they are. I was both terrified and in denial simultane-ously. I heard Pastor Donnie say that he didn't want to go to the hospital. I have some much reverence for my pastors, how could I tell them what to do?! Instead I tried to take care of them to the best of my ability.

I left that night feeling uneasy. I really didn't like the way they looked. I prayed they would be okay. I decided to come back the following night. That night my pastors looked even worse. I had brought every over the counter item I could think of that might help them. While I was there I thought, could this be COVID-19? I pushed those thoughts out of my head and focused on caring for them. I heard Pastor Sara suggest that they go to the hospital since they were only getting worse. I sheepishly said "yeah" to the idea of going to the hospital. However, Pastor Donnie insisted that he wanted to stay home. Once again, how could I even think of overruling my precious humble Pastors?! The answer was simple. I couldn't. Pastor Sara stated that if they were not feeling better by tomorrow, that they would both go to the hospital. I was relieved by that idea.

That night I went home again after Pastor Sara promised to call me in the morning to let me know how they were doing. That night I was very restless. I woke up several times concerned about my pastors. That morning I got a call from Pastor Sara. I enthusi-astically answered the phone and waited with bated breath for good news. However, that's not what I heard. Pastor Sara stated "Paige, we need to go to the hospital. Take your time, get ready and come over". My heart sunk. Even in the midst of illness my Pastor still wanted me to take time for myself. Their love and com-passion is so heartfelt. I got ready as fast as I could and rushed to their house.

When I got to their house they both appeared toxically ill. Even worse than the night prior when I had last seen them. Pastor Donnie was having visible rigors and constant coughing. He was obviously septic. Pastor Sara looked ill too.

As soon as I got there I called 911. Within minutes we had a first responder from the fire department. Unfortunately, his tone was demeaning and disingenuous. One of the first things he said was "turn off the humidifier" which Is a reasonable request because Covid-19 can aerosolizes with humidifiers. Once he found out that I was a medical provider, He immediately assumed that I was inappropriately keeping my parents out of the hospital and trying to treat them at home. He also told the arriving EMS theses unfortunate assumptions despite not being told this. When I requested that my parents be sent to a specific hospital he condescendingly rebuffed my request, then followed his statement with "don't come" to the hospital they aren't letting anyone inside. While I understand that he was only following protocols, his lack of empathy and curt tone only made a bad situation feel even worse.

Pastor Sara insisted that Pastor Donnie take the first ambulance that arrived because he was the sickest. It was heartbreaking to watch Pastor Donnie attempt to stand up from the sofa by himself. He at that moment looked frail, he was visible shaking/rigoring and required assistance to get onto the stretcher. The next ambulance arrived moments later and took my Pastor Sara. I stood outside and watched EMS take my parents. When they left, I just sat down and cried. I was instructed not to go to the hospital. However, there was no way I could just sit there and not try. I drove to the hospital and parked in the visitor parking lot. While walking to the ER bay I saw the dispatched fire fighter and the EMS driver standing outside in the ambulance bay. I watched as the dispatched fire fighter nudged the EMS guy to look in my direction and they both glared at me as I walked towards the ER.

A lady donned in scrubs and a mask stood up and greeted me at the door blocking my entrance into the ER. I asked her if my parents had been registered yet. She instructed me to call the hospital to find out. I said I'm standing right here, is there any way you can just tell me if my dad has been admitted yet? I only see one out of the two ambulances that transported my family to the hospital. She reluctantly agreed to check to see if they had been registered. A few moments later she said that my dad Donnie Price was there and my mom had just arrived. That put me slightly at ease. She then reminded me again that there was a strict no visitor policy due to the covid-19 outbreak. I more than understood. This is the same protocol that all hospitals had been adhering to for weeks by this time. The rules are in place to protect patients and their families. I knew better. However, it didn't make me feel any better. It was so hard letting go.

I walked back to the car defeated. I didn't dear look at the ambulance bay because I didn't want to give any credence to the firefighters warning. He was right, I couldn't get it. I couldn't be with my family when they needed me the most. I became that desperate family member who needed to be comforted, consoled and just told that everything was going to be okay. For the first time since I become a medical provider, I was on the outside of the hospital trying to looking in. Little did I know, the battle just begun.

Gratefully, the ER doctor called me within 2 hours. He told me that my dad was going to be admitted to the hospital. He told me my dad was very sick. He asked me how I felt about my mom coming home because she wasn't as sick. I spoke to my mom about it and then called the ER doctor back and told him that we would feel safer if she was at least observed overnight. Gratefully, the ER doctor was receptive and had both of my parents admitted.

I was told that they both had pneumonia present on admission and within 24 hours of admission they both tested positive for COVID-19. My dad was septic on admission. Meaning that he met hospital criteria for being very ill when he arrived.

During this whole ordeal I was so consumed with everything going on around me that I barely noticed how poorly I felt. I was having upper respiratory symptoms and having chills. I don't own a thermometer (I know as a provider that I probably should) but I felt like I was having fevers also. I reported my symptoms and I got tested for coronavirus. My test came back positive too.

Then I started to worry. Since I was working with Covid-19 patients in the hospital, did I infect my family? Was this all my fault? The guilt was unbearable. I had adhered to all the safety protocols and always wore all the available PPE. Still the possibility of me being possibly culpable was devastating.

I'm neurotic about how I take care of my patients at work and my parents aren't an exception to this rule. I tried my best to spoke to the RN/medical providers daily so I could be abreast with my families' condition.

Gratefully, Pastor Sara improved rapidly. Within 3 days she was back home praising the Lord. We continued to recover from COVID-19. We both were still experiencing some upper respiratory symptoms along with fatigue. We started to pray and intercede for Pastor Donnie. We were determined to ignore any negativity thrown our way.

Back in the hospital, It was hard to hear my dad get sicker and sicker every day without being able to do anything for him. My siblings when we called would only speak to him for a few minutes at a time because it was too hard for him to speak and breathe simultaneously. For approximately the first 7-9 days, he continuously spiked fevers, his inflammatory markers continued to rise daily, his oxygen level continued to drop and he started to show signs of heart and liver injury which can happen with COVID-19 patients. I inquired about starting him on hydrochloriquine, they only medication that showed any promise in trials at that time. Three days later, he was started on hydroxyhloriquine and he started to improve. My family and I were so grateful. However, his journey was far from over.

24 hours after he was admitted he was started on antibiotics for pneumonia. They told me one of his antibiotics for pneumonia needed to be stopped early because they were going to start hydrochloroquine due to potential interactions. He initially started to do better once it was started and the entire family was relieved.

On April 11th at 3 am my mother and I both woke up at the same time. This never happens. We decided to call the hospital and check on dad. The nurse came to the phone. He told me that he paged the doctor twice because my dad was having difficulty breathing several times. The doctor had ordered diuretics but they weren't helping. I requested that the nurse call the doctor again to see my dad.

A few hours later I get the gut-wrenching call from the nocturnist. He tells me he is moving my dad to the ICU due to his worsening respiratory status. There really isn't much that can prepare you to receive this call. I've told patients numerous times that their family members were being transferred to the ICU. While it's never easy for a provider to call and give this type of update to a family member, it is far worse to be on the receiving end. I reluctantly gave this information to my mom.

In the ICU, antibiotics were resumed for his pneumonia and his hydroxycloquine was continued. Due to the severity of his symptoms he was started on IV steroids which are sometimes given to severely ill patients especially while in the ICU. He had a few tenuous days where they were planning on intubating him, but by the grace of God he didn't require intubation. He stated that whenever they came into the room prepared to intubate him due to worsening hypoxia. He would pray harder and would muster up enough strength to say "I'm fine" and try to "pretend" that he was breathing okay by attempting to control his breathing. At one point he was up to 10 liters of oxygen while they were preparing to intubate him. He later told us that he knew that if he didn't control his breathing that they would've intubated him and he would've lost control of the situation.

By the grace of God, after 2.5-3 days in the ICU he was transferred back to the medical floor. They did a chest CT at that time which the ICU doctor confirmed the presence of covid-19 related pneumonia, bacterial pneumonia, mild heart failure and it revealed a new finding, a pulmonary embolism.

He not only had Pneumonia, Covid-19, mucous plugging, signs/symptoms of heart failure but now he also has a pulmonary embolism. By medical criteria he met criteria for severe illness. Even though he was out of the ICU, he wasn't out of the woods yet. While the fevers have started to subside. He continued to be hypoxic every morning.

Pastor Sara and I continued to pray and fast for Donnie. A few days went bye and he continued to get stronger and stronger. His morning episodes of hypoxia especially with coughing started to improve. Physical therapy initially recommended rehab, but he improved so rapidly that he didn't qualify for rehabilitation as he started to improve so quickly. They told us He barely met criteria for oxygen on discharge.

After 2 weeks of being hospitalized, we finally got the call that he was ready to come home. We were ecstatic. When he picked him up from the hospital I barely recognized my dad. "Welcome home!" we yelled as they released my dad to us via the ER entrance via a wheelchair. My dad looked gaunt and malnourished. He had lost at least 20 lbs. He definitely looked better than when he went in, but he still appeared sick. He looked at us but there wasn't any hint of recognition in his eyes. His once cheerful disposition had vanished.

Once home he had tenuous days battling hypoxia, shortness of breath and ongoing respiratory symptoms that led to respiratory distress. There were mornings where he would wake up in respiratory distress and his oxygen level would be in the 70s while on oxygen and it would take him a very long time to recover. His morning episodes of hypoxia were persistent for weeks. Seeing your family in respiratory distress and being unsure if you can help them has been the most traumatizing experience of my life. During some of his hypoxic /respiratory distress episodes I was unsure if he was going to recover at all. As a medical provider I was worrying if I was doing the right thing. Should we bring him back to the hospital due to ongoing episodes of respiratory distress? Are we doing the right thing by keeping him home? Am I being negligent? Through it all, Pastor Donnie made us promise not to bring him back to the hospital and we were determined to keep our promise.

Pastor Donnie didn't only have medical sequeala from his hospitalization; he also appeared to be experiencing emotional sequela as well. He was emotionally withdrawn and appeared to be experiencing PTSD. I never realized how traumatizing the hospital experience can be on patients. As providers, we tend to focus on the medical aspect of patient care, neglecting the emotional elements. It took some time, but Pastor Donnie gradually started opening up regarding his hospitalization.

Most importantly, Pastor Donnie continued to hold onto the anchor which is Jesus Christ and it was beautiful to see the Lord heal him completely. This experience was truly humbling. It was a reminder that all things through Jesus Christ are possible. He is the Lord that health thee. In the face of adversity never give up hope. Pastor Donnie went from being severely ill in a hospital bed in the ICU with a poor prognosis, to being home healed by the Grace of God.

Pastor Donnie continued to hold onto the anchor which is Jesus Christ even when his situation looked dire. The Lord continued to reveal himself beautifully to Pastor Donnie during his hospitalization and comforted him. He never lost focused through it all. We are truly grateful to the Lord for healing our entire family. Pastor Sara, Pastor Donnie and myself are all survivors of the coronavirus thanks to the Grace of God.

If for some reason the Lord takes your loved one home, ask the Lord for the strength to endure. This takes a lot of prayer and it's not always easy. Even when it is difficult try to remember romans 8:18 *For I reckon that the sufferings of this present time are not worthy to be compared with the glory which shall be revealed in us*. Remember we will see all of our saved Loved ones again who rest in Christ.

About the Author

Apostle/Pastor /Evangelist /Chaplain/CEO/president of Power in Prayer Worldwide Outreach Ministries, Sara Jane Price, has dedicated her whole life to the Lord's work. She gave her heart to Jesus Christ at the age of six years. She was handing out gospel tracks on the street at age eight years.

She traveled and was under her dad, Rev Billy Watson's ministry all of her life until the Lord promoted her for Worldwide Outreach Ministry called Power in Prayer. Apostle Sara has started two churches, one in Richmond, Virginia, and one in Wareham, Massachusetts, training in discipleship and teaching leaders to follow their gifts and callings. God had used her to pray over the city council meetings in Richmond, Virginia.

She has set her own Gospel Tents for over thirty years. And she calls the tent The Ark of Jesus.

She has seen so many people healed and set free and delivered and so many miracles in their lives. God has used her to preach in the prisons, nursing homes, hospitals, auditoriums, and on the streets. And God uses her to feed the poor, care for them, and love them.

She has held so many conferences about the books of Revelation and Daniel, and all about the end time.

She's also an end-time messenger for the last days before the return of Jesus Christ. She loves Jesus Christ very much. Sara has a great love for her family and her husband Donnie Price of forty-eight years. She loves to be a homemaker and loves to cook. She really enjoys her grandbaby and plays basketball, fishing, and riding on the four-wheeler.

She loves playing Her B3 Hammond organ and she also loves to sing southern gospel.

God has used her to pour gallons of anointed oil in so many states. She declared the land back to God. And God has used her to anoint the capital in Washington, DC. God has used her in Africa and India and across the nations. She has a love for Israel, and she supports Israel. God has used her for many years in fasting and praying out in the woods. God has shown her a great visitation of heaven and hell, the white throne judgment, and much more. God has use her in television/radio and interviews with the newspapers.

She believes in the power of God and the spoken Word of God and the power of intercessory prayer. God has used her, and she has even seen the dead risen in her ministry. She believes in the power of prayer, and she believes in faith that God can do anything but fail. Her motto is she cannot do anything, but she pitches out the barrels of the anointing, and He does all the work, and He gets all the glory. God has used her to travel thousands and thousands of miles to spread the Gospel and win many souls for the kingdom of God. God had used her to preach to many nationalities. "

Apostle Sara J. Price was born in Beckley, West Virginia, to the Reverend William and Margaret Watson.

She is a licensed, ordained minister under ICC Ministries Dr. Michael Chitwood of Chattanooga, Tennessee, and a registered chaplain under Dr. Ronnie Shaw Chattanooga Tennessee She's also ordained, and licensed under the ministry under Rev H. Richard Hall of Cleveland, Tennessee.

Picture of Sara and Donnie under Her Gospel Tent

If you need prayer, just email
pipworldwideoutreachsjp@gmail.com

She does a prayer meeting by phone, called the Warrior Bride every Monday at 7 p.m.

If you would like to invite her to come to your churches and speak on the miracles and what happened with the COVID-19 and many other miracles, please contact Pastor Sara. She would also do a conference in your church, teaching on the books of Revelation and Daniel. She would also be happy to tell your church the vision she had going to heaven and of a vision she had seeing heaven and hell and the white throne judgment.

When your church needs an old-fashioned gospel revival, God uses her in signs and wonders and also the word of knowledge, the spoken Word of God over your life. Her church is located at 181 Main Street, Wareham, Massachusetts. Everyone is welcome on Sunday mornings at 10:30 a.m. If you would like to sponsor her or donate, please write her feel free at:

Power in Prayer Sara J Price
P.O. Box 959
Wareham, Mass 02571

CPSIA information can be obtained
at www.ICGtesting.com
Printed in the USA
LVHW021232251120
672429LV00006B/8